T0029555

SMALL
TALK

SMALL TALK

10 ADHD lies and how to stop believing them

RICHARD & ROXANNE PINK

TEN SPEED PRESS
California | New York

This book is a work of non-fiction based on the lives, experiences, and recollections of the authors. In some cases names of people, places, dates, sequences, and the detail of events have been changed to protect the privacy of others. This book aims to provide useful information based on the authors' personal experience, but it is not intended to replace your doctor's medical advice.

2024 Ten Speed Trade Paperback Edition

Copyright © 2024 by Richard Pink and Roxanne Pink

All rights reserved.
Published in the United States by Ten Speed Press, an imprint of the Crown Publishing Group, a division of Penguin Random House LLC, New York.
tenspeed.com
crownpublishing.com

Ten Speed Press and the Ten Speed Press colophon are registered trademarks of Penguin Random House LLC.

Originally published in the United Kingdom by Square Peg, an imprint of Vintage, a division of Penguin Random House UK, in 2024.

Library of Congress Control Number: 2024935644

Trade Paperback ISBN: 978-0-593-83699-6
eBook ISBN: 978-0-593-83700-9

Printed in the United States on acid-free paper

Acquiring editor: Molly Birnbaum
Project editor: Gabby Ureña Matos
Production editor: Sohayla Farman
Production designer: Mari Gill
Production manager: Dan Myers
Publicist: Kristin Casemore
Marketer: Brianne Sperber

10 9 8 7 6 5 4 3 2 1

Contents

SMALL TALK

The Book That Almost Didn't Exist

Written by Rox

Hi, I'm Rox. The majority of the internet now knows me as the "ADHD Wife."

But, long before this, I had another name—a not-very-nice one I gave myself somewhere between almost getting kicked out of university and quitting my first job as a trainee accountant. The use of *first* here is very important. You see, I have bailed on *lots* of jobs. And some half-decent relationships. And some potentially money-making business ideas. And some life-changing wellness journeys. And in fact, the first draft of this book . . .

It was a rather lovely manuscript, full of advice about how to thrive with ADHD. We were fifty research hours, three chapters and a million cover design ideas deep when I decided to start over. Explaining to Rich (my partner and co-author of this book!) that six months' worth of work was being thrown away on what looked like a whim was an interesting conversation . . . I was met with his usual brand of quiet contemplation, curiosity and advice. But after he listened to why I felt we needed to change direction, he agreed.

Let me back up for a moment. The reason why we originally decided to write this book was quite simply . . . you. The people who we are lucky enough to be connected to via social media. In a world where such platforms are often used to divide, we found a community of people who just wanted to feel like they weren't alone in their struggles. Who could for the first time say, "Wait, so it isn't just me who always forgets the laundry in the dryer?" People who were eager to learn that perhaps they weren't terrible humans, but rather people with a neuro-developmental condition . . .

Halfway through our second book idea (RIP), I asked a question to our @ADHD_Love followers: "What are some core beliefs that you hold about yourself?" I was hoping to gather some information for an uplifting chapter on neurodivergent identity. But as I began reading the replies, my heart sank:

> *I am lazy.*
> *I'm not trying hard enough.*
> *I quit everything I start.*
> *I am stupid.*
> *ADHD isn't real.*
> *Everybody secretly hates me.*
> *I am useless.*
> *I am a burden.*
> *I am a failure.*
> *The world would be better off without me.*

There were over 5,000 replies. Every single one was as gut-wrenching as the last. I realised that our community has a huge and deep-seated problem: a shocking level of self-hatred. Suddenly our book on neuro-divergent self-discipline (featuring tips like "using scented candles to stay focused") felt like a bandage on a bullet hole.

What the hell, I asked myself, is the point of telling people how to be more productive when they ABSOLUTELY HATE THEMSELVES? What does success even mean if people are walking around believing they are utterly unlovable? What point is there to organization if you don't even feel worthy of being alive?

There are so many books, podcasts and articles out there advising people with ADHD on how to be more productive. Some of them are incredibly helpful. But my God . . . There is a bigger problem we have to talk about. And that is that many neurodivergent people are living with crippling, toxic core beliefs. Beliefs that they have internalised so deeply that they override every good thing about them. Beliefs put there by a world that is not built for them. Beliefs put there by the harsh words of critics, teachers, and perhaps more painfully, parents and loved ones. Beliefs that, if not weeded out and replaced, will inform the rest of their lives.

Perhaps this is a good time for me to actually get to the point, and tell you about my former name. The one I used to call myself for many years. It was:

LAZY. USELESS. LOSER.

Okay, so it's three names. Or perhaps a first name and a double-barrel surname.

Hi, I'm Lazy Useless-Loser. Nice to meet you.

I haven't called myself this in quite some time . . . but reading your replies brought it all flooding right back. For a very long time, I believed so many toxic things—lies—about myself. My inner narrative used to sound like this:

- When I lost something: "*You are disgusting and careless.*"
- When I was late to something: "*You disrespectful mess.*"

3

- When I was melting down: "*You attention-seeking child.*"
- When I quit something: "*You fucking failure.*"

I now call this "small talk." Talking down to yourself. Speaking to yourself as if you are worthless, ensuring you continue to play small. Of course, we neurodivergents know the other kind of small talk . . . the insufferable conversation starters we are meant to have with everybody that we meet—which can feel boring to downright terrifying. Just another skill we failed to learn, along with how to keep on top of the cleaning or how to stop getting bored of a new hobby. Fear not . . . this book is literally the total opposite of *that* type of small talk. It's deep, heavy, and in fact should probably come with a trigger warning or two. So here it is. Consider yourself warned. Big Talk only in these pages, which will include looking at addiction, trauma, self-harm and family relationships. (All much better than talking about the weather, if you ask me . . .)

Back to the horrible inner narrative that I used to live with. As I explained in our first book, *Dirty Laundry*, until my mid-thirties, I had been living with a lot of unprocessed trauma and undiagnosed ADHD—a recipe for disaster. And without the language to understand what was happening, the only thing I could do was blame myself. I was my own personal fear-leading squad, spewing negativity over every inch of my life on a continuous loop.

I was an alcoholic, a relationship addict, $50,000 in debt and living in spare rooms. My only certainty was the belief I would never amount to anything in life. It was too late for me; I was a lazy, useless loser. I was destined to sit in a pub, bitterly lamenting my wasted potential over a pint for years to come.

But then I did a 180. At the age of 34, I got sober. I'd absolutely love to tell you that one day I woke up and decided it was time to get better.

As with most addicts though . . . the decision to turn things around was not that easy. I had to hit rock bottom. The absolute worst moment in my life. A three-day bender. A relationship breakdown. A shit ton of debt. And even more self-hatred. I walked into my first recovery meeting, and within an hour, my time as the "life and soul" of the party was over. And thank God for that.

That first year sober was brutal. All of the emotions I had been numbing my whole life came back with a vengeance. I confronted the grief of losing my mum, the fact that I was in so much debt, and that I had never been able to maintain a relationship, or a job. I was deeply ashamed of the life I had lived up until then, and couldn't see a way out. Life without red wine was so intolerable to me, that it sent me into therapy, where I have been for the last four years. It's then I made the discovery that I have ADHD (more on that later). That self-knowledge changed EVERYTHING.

Because, you see, even sober, I *still* suffered with "small talk"—*still* thought I was a useless piece of shit. But being diagnosed with ADHD meant I had to force myself to see my life and my struggles differently. The four years since my diagnosis have been a journey to change my core beliefs and stop believing awful lies about myself. To find my truth—which is that perhaps I wasn't and am not the worst person alive, but someone in desperate need of more support. When I started changing the way I spoke to myself, my life began to change dramatically.

I learned that you can't build a life you love when you hate yourself. Our inner talk is like a compass, determining whether or not we'll find happiness, or at least acceptance. If our inner-talk is toxic, if it's all fearleader and no cheerleader, it will drag us down, take us to dark places, and sabotage our best efforts to find joy. That core belief is like

True North. And we will always find it. So . . . how can we change that compass setting from pointing out our failures, and direct ourselves to somewhere better? How do we stop believing all these horrible things about ourselves?

Often, the missing setting on that compass is not willpower, or trying harder: it's understanding. Acceptance. Support. And love. I wonder how many of you are blaming yourselves for things that are not within your control, willing yourselves to change, when what you really need is a cup of tea, a warm hug and someone to tell you that you matter deeply. That your past does not define your future. And that you deserve to be treated with respect and kindness. By others, *and* by yourself.

I hope this book can be that.* A cup of tea. A warm hug. And a road map out of self-hatred. I know it's possible. And I know it can change your life.

* (P.S. I also truly hope you don't think this book is shit, because it would be really awkward after we threw the other one away.)

Writing a Book With My ADHD Wife

Written by Rich

Writing a book is hard. Writing a book with someone who has ADHD is . . . umm . . . *interesting*.

For me, writing is simply about finding the time to do it. My process is as follows:

1. Pick a date we're both free.
2. Block it out in the diary.
3. Make sure we have a constant flow of caffeine.
4. Brainstorm a chapter.
5. Write the chapter.

Efficient. And extremely unlikely for us to be able to achieve.

You see, Rox's method for writing goes something like this:

1. Wait for a random burst of energy and inspiration.
2. Start writing even if it's 11.30 p.m. or we are meant to be going out in ten minutes.

My desire for order was constantly bumping into her desire for freedom and creativity. I'd block out a day in both of our diaries for us to write, only to find out on the day itself that Rox had agreed to meet a friend in London, and that she'd only added our writing date to her "mind calendar" rather than our shared digital one.

Or we'd drive to a lovely location so we could focus on typing up chapter notes, only for Rox to say she didn't have the energy to work. We made many a trip to Homebase (the UK equivalent for Home Depot in the US) for whiteboards so we could lay out chapter titles, only for Rox to fill them with ideas for Etsy businesses and random doodles.

But we eventually found a way to make it work. I ploughed through my research and writing on a strict schedule. Rox wrote when she felt inspired. And we pieced it together, giving each other feedback and encouragement along the way. We had a deadline to meet with our publisher for the first few chapters of our book, and I was delighted (and perhaps a little surprised) that we actually made it. First chapters were sent off, and the book cover was being designed. Lovely. We were on the way to finishing our second book!

The day after delivering our first few chapters, however, Rox walked into our bedroom looking upset.

"Babe," she said, "I need to speak to you about the book."

I resisted the urge to pull out my hair as she proceeded to tell me that she no longer wanted to write this book and, in fact, wanted to start again on a totally different idea.

Internally, my initial response was, "You must be joking. It's taken six months to write three chapters. We haven't got time." But instead, I said, "Tell me more."

I have learned to be "open to a different experience" (to borrow from our therapist) and hear Rox out when she is very passionate about something, because there can often be genius in her ideas. Sometimes, as with any of us, there's total nonsense. But occasionally there are nuggets of pure gold. So, I nervously asked her why the change of heart.

Arms waving around like a mad scientist, pyjama-clad and passionate, she proceeded to pitch me the new idea. Something about social media. Something about core beliefs. Something about ADHD people hating themselves. Something about rewriting the entire thing.

"The worst symptom of ADHD isn't what we all think it is! It's not the losing things, memory issues, hobby swapping, or overwhelm . . . it's actually the horrible beliefs we have developed about ourselves from living with these symptoms in a world that doesn't accommodate us. We need to write a book about the core beliefs holding our community back. Not a productivity book. Please."

Of course, it crossed my mind to say no. To heavily encourage that we stick to our original idea. To make a list about why this didn't make sense. But I decided against it for two reasons. Firstly, getting Rox to do something she isn't emotionally invested in anymore would be like dragging her through tar. And secondly, I could see the *magic* in her. That magic is the glint in her eye and the crazy hand movements that tell me she believes this idea is heaven-sent. It was the side quest of all side quests. And hey, who am I to disagree with that oh-so-convincing ADHD intuition?

After a night's sleep and some time to digest the possibility of throwing our productivity book away and starting again, something hit me. A memory of Rox in our first year together. She was getting ready for a music video shoot I was driving her to. She'd decided not to get ready the night before (absolutely not a shock), so the morning was a bit of a mad rush.

She was trying on clothes and nothing seemed to be going right. The pile of discarded outfits on the floor was growing, and her face was getting redder and redder.

"Babe, are you okay?" I asked her.

"No . . ." I could hear the mixture of panic and pain in her shaking voice. "I'm a stupid fucking idiot. Why have I left it so late? I cannot be trusted to get anything right." And then she broke down in tears.

The next hour was a rescue mission of repairing tear-smudged mascara and finding a good-enough outfit. We got everything together and made it to the video on time. Rox's neurotypical mask went on, well practised over years of having to pretend she was okay when she wasn't, and the shoot went very well. But I was still very shaken by the heaviness of her words and her perceived "failure" as a human—simply for not having picked out her clothes the night before.

After the video I decided to raise it with her.

"Babe," I began, "I know you were super frustrated, but the way you spoke to yourself this morning was really nasty."

"What do you mean?" She looked genuinely confused.

"Calling yourself stupid, and swearing at yourself."

"Oh . . . that!" She laughed. "That is pretty much what it sounds like in my head all the time. I just said it out loud today."

It was the first time she had ever shared with me—or anyone else—the constant bullying that she was living with, the cruel voice inside her head. To her, it was normal. To me, it was horrendous. I felt almost ill to think that the person that I love, a person I know to be kind, caring and empathetic, was living with a constant loop of self-abuse in her own head. We had to put a stop to it.

Over the next few years, we began to work together on her self-talk, with regular reminders from me of when she was being mean and needed to apologise to herself. I am well aware this sounds a bit crazy, but put it this way: if anyone spoke to you that way, you would expect an apology, right?

We now refer to this kind of language as "small talk."

A combination of therapy and a very attuned home environment meant things started to get better for Rox. Her inner narrative began to change from one of personal failure and "not-good-enough-ness" to one of kindness and compassion. Now, a lost wallet still stings a bit, but she can say, "Ahhh, that's so frustrating. Guess the ADHD is ADHD-ing," rather than "I am a horrible person and I never do anything right."

Overall, the lens of ADHD has allowed Rox to crawl out from under the rock of self-hatred. It's given her language and explanations for some of her biggest struggles. She has also gone on to do some pretty amazing things in life and work, things I know she previously believed to be impossible.

Every person deserves this: the freedom to understand that their struggles mean they deserve support, *not* shame and judgment. The good news is that partners, parents and friends can be a vital part of helping someone with ADHD achieve that freedom.

This is the idea that resonated with Rox.

She has walked in these shoes. She has hated herself for years. She knows where this kind of thinking leads.

And this is why we had to write this book. A book that isn't about changing you. But rather making you realise you are pretty awesome just as you are. The biggest change I ever saw in Rox was when she learned to change her core beliefs. So that's what we want to help you to do as well. Goodbye productivity book. Hello let's-kick-those-nasty-negative-core-beliefs-in-the-ass book.

If you are lucky enough to love someone with ADHD, you will no doubt have heard them speak horribly to themselves. You'll know how easily shame overcomes them, and that believing they are broken, disliked or at fault is their natural setting. It is our job, as people who love them, to reflect back their value, call out the self-bullying, and help them to rebuild their lost self-esteem.

Throughout this book, we will tackle the most toxic core beliefs of people with ADHD. We call them the ADHD Lies. As with our previous book, we'll do it through two lenses: from Rox's perspective, as someone who has lived with these beliefs for many years and finally found a way to change them. And from my perspective, as someone who has supported her, helped her, and encouraged her every step of the way. We will share (well, perhaps overshare!) how each one of the ADHD Lies has affected us, and how we have worked to stop believing them.

Thank you so much for choosing to spend this time with us. It truly is a pleasure to get to speak directly to you, and I really hope that you find support in these pages.*

* Of course, there's a chance this book ends up in a to-be-read pile that you never actually get to, but if that's NOT the case, and if you are holding it right now, know that it was the product of an ADHD-inspired change in direction, many late nights of hyperfocus, and a deep desire to help folks with ADHD to become all that they truly can be.

Small Talk: 10 ADHD Lies

Written by Rich and Rox

In popular psychology, a core belief is a deeply held, unshakeable conviction about how we understand ourselves and the world around us. Core beliefs drive our behaviour, thoughts and emotions. Core beliefs can also become self-fulfilling prophecies: often, we hold onto them so tightly that our actions, often subconsciously, bring about evidence that our beliefs are true.

Imagine someone who holds the core belief, "I am deserving of love and respect." This person is likelier to meet others with confidence and know how to set boundaries. This person has an internal compass that will alert them to exploitative or emotionally unsafe situations. They are likelier to sense if something is off about a prospective partner, and view disrespect as an immediate red flag. They are likelier to take action to get away from whatever is causing deep unease.

Unfortunately, the reverse is also true. If someone holds the core belief, "I am unworthy of love and respect," they will view themselves as less than others, and may spend a lot of time and energy trying to prove their worth. They are more likely to be in abusive relationships, be easily taken advantage of at work, and find it difficult to see red flags. Being treated poorly may actually feel familiar, if not correct, to them—like something they deserve.

People with ADHD and AuDHD (autism and ADHD) are far more susceptible to developing toxic core beliefs.[1] There are several reasons for this:

1. The average ADHDer receives 20,000 times more negative feedback than those without ADHD by the age of 10.[2]
2. ADHDers are more likely to be disciplined and rejected by parents.
3. ADHDers are more likely to struggle and be singled out at school.
4. ADHDers are more likely to struggle with maintaining friendships.
5. ADHDers are more likely to struggle to maintain a job.
6. ADHDers are more likely to struggle with "basic" tasks such as cleaning, time management and organization.

In this book, we will discuss the ten most damaging of these beliefs, which we call the 10 ADHD Lies. We will help you to notice them for what they are, and we'll help you to recognise which lies are affecting your life, how to stop believing them, and to find some much kinder core beliefs. Ones that will protect and inspire you or a loved one with ADHD.

We will share stories from our own lives—from our childhood and adolescence to our current relationship. Of course, we are aware that every ADHD experience is unique, and we do not intend to speak for everyone. But we hope that you will identify with some of what we share, and can begin to embark on the same journey of healing that we've undertaken.

The 10 ADHD Lies we'll discuss were taken directly from our community. Some of them are incredibly difficult to read. But we believe it's important to walk headfirst into these tough conversations in order to dismantle the beliefs behind them and begin to recover.

To put it another way, simply trying to force yourself to be more productive, better with time, and more focused is pointless if you believe that, at heart, you are some kind of broken, worthless, horrible person. You'll be working from a place of punishment, as opposed to one of self-acceptance and healing. Trying to change our behaviour without first changing our core beliefs is like building a house on sand: the foundations are not steady. No matter what we build, the minute the tide comes in, that house will be washed away. A house built on solid ground, however, can weather life's many storms.

And that is what we want to get at in this book—that your core beliefs are your foundation. And if those beliefs are positive, strong and inspiring, whatever you build on top of them will have a greater chance of actually working.

So, let's get started. Let's drag each of those toxic ADHD lies out into the light of day, expose them for the hateful nonsense they are, and replace them with something positive and solid that you can begin to (re)build on.

Ready? Take a deep breath. And let's get into it.

It's time to reprogramme who you believe you are at your very core. (See . . . we told you it wasn't going to be "small talk!")

All the love,
Rich and Rox

ADHD Lie #1: I Am Lazy

Written by Rox

For the majority of my adult life, I would have sworn that I was lazy. It was the only word in the English language that summed up my consistent lack of action in the face of things that needed to get done. Missed deadlines. Missed opportunities. Everything left to the last minute. A messy home. Late bills. Countless failed attempts to get healthy. And a graveyard of unrealised creative dreams. Like Sherlock Holmes on a mission to persecute himself, I'd been collecting evidence of my inherent laziness from a very young age . . .

When I was 9, I started my first business, Helping Hands.

I designed a flyer on Microsoft Word—a bright green logo and a jpeg of two joined hands. (The fact I can remember this flyer in vivid detail but often have no idea why I've walked into a room is very on-brand!) I added a list of things I would be able to help with for the price of $6 an hour.

- gardening
- car cleaning
- house cleaning
- washing up

One new ink cartridge later, I was off on a walk around our neighbourhood to distribute my little flyers. The sun was shining and I was filled with the joys of possibility! Although there were no phone calls in the first couple of days, I didn't lose hope. I knew *someone* was going to want my help. The flyer was too delicious to ignore.

Three days later, the first phone call came.

"Hi! We live at number eight. We're going away for a week and we'd love for you to take care of our rabbit, Prince."

My first job!

Before my neighbours left for their holiday, I visited their house. Down our driveway, ten steps to the right on a quiet cul-de-sac, and then I was there. It was an exceptionally simple walk to work. I had my notepad and pen with me, and took extraordinarily thorough notes on how to take care of the slightly chubby, slightly smelly, but absolutely adorable rabbit.

On the first day of their trip, I arrived early, eager to begin. I completed my checklist in record time, and left with a sense of real achievement. I was a pre-teen entrepreneur on my way to earning my first $42.

But on day two, something had changed. I didn't feel any motivation to go and look after Prince. I knew I needed to go, but somehow couldn't get my feet to move. I was in a prison of my own making. I left it so late that my bedtime was approaching. My dad, petrified that I might kill the rabbit, sternly reminded me that I had to go, offering to walk with me. This pattern continued for the next five days until our neighbours came home. Extraordinarily thankful this awful task was over, I promptly closed my business and threw away the rest of the Helping Hands flyers.

I was ashamed of my behaviour. It made no sense. Who asks for a job and then doesn't do it? There's something wrong with me, I thought. What a lazy kid.

What I *didn't* think about was the good aspects of my project, short-lived as it had been:

I never thought about the creativity of my original idea.

I never thought about the skills involved in designing a flyer.

I never thought about my optimism in the face of no phone calls.

All I thought about was how lazy and awful I must be. To go to all this effort to get a job, and then not want to do it. To force my dad to remind me, and for him to have to walk with me to make sure I got the job done. What a letdown. What a loser.

Although I closed my fledgling company after my experience with the rabbit formerly known as Prince, the legacy of Helping Hands lived on for the next three decades of my life. I was full of great ideas, and terrible execution. This could affect something as large as a new business idea, or as small as a desire to get on top of my washing. I would decide I wanted to do something, believe wholeheartedly I could do it, and then fail. Again and again. When thousands of good intentions result in thousands of failures, there is only one answer to the question, "What the hell is happening?" And that answer is that I am lazy. I was still a long way from my ADHD diagnosis, and this was the first lie I ever told myself.

ADHD people are often judged as lazy because they struggle with things like laundry, taxes or small talk (the mundane chit-chat kind). The boring tasks. And I can completely understand why a neurotypical person who also didn't enjoy these jobs would shout from the rooftops, "You're just lazy!" I mean . . . who really wants to do those things?! Unless you have sat and stared at a task willing yourself to get up and start working, and bursting out into tears because no matter how hard you will yourself to work, your body doesn't seem to move, it's going to be quite hard to understand the ADHD struggle.

In our house we call losing motivation for a task "notivation." **Notivation** means having no motivation for a low-dopamine task. Feeling notivated (yes, it's an actual verb now!) for boring tasks makes sense, but what about when it applies to something that you love and really want to do? That's the thing with ADHD—it doesn't just come for the cleaning and the organizing. It can also come for your dreams and your passions.

This is something I experienced most of my life. And then, when I was 36 years old, I learned an incredible new term that explained pretty much all of my struggles: **executive dysfunction**. I was floored. After three decades of screaming "Lazy!" at myself, I suddenly had a scientific-sounding explanation for why I had been struggling to complete certain tasks.

Here's a brief explanation from the UK's ADHD Centre:

"Executive dysfunction is a brain-based impairment that causes problems with analyzing, planning, organizing, scheduling, and completing tasks at all—or on deadline."[3]

According to the organization, if you struggle with executive dysfunction, you will find difficulties in the following areas:

- Time management
- Organizational skills
- Multitasking
- Working memory and remembering things
- Planning
- Prioritising tasks

- Paying attention
- Regulating emotions
- Self-censoring

I don't believe in magic, but this discovery felt as if somebody had waved a wand and broken the "lazy curse." Suddenly the reason why I could be brought to my knees by a pile of laundry could be explained. The puzzle pieces started falling into place: the reason behind why I always lived in a mess, fell behind on taxes, got overwhelmed by the simplest task, or couldn't follow through on a commitment—all was explained.

When the "I am lazy" record stops playing in your head it creates a lot of space. Space for a new understanding of what hard work means when you have ADHD.

My ethos around "working hard" looks different to the standard view of eight hours a day, highly organized, planned down to the minute. Instead, I work in huge bursts of creative energy, making the most of my hyperfocus hours, and I also rest a lot. I rest more than the average person, but I also multiply my productivity tenfold when I work from an inspired and motivated place.

And to my astonishment, I've discovered that I am actually extremely hard-working; it is just a very different type of hard work than the norm. I had been so focused on the fact I was lazy, I had totally overlooked it!

I need rest to maximise my productivity when motivation strikes, and I am capable of huge amounts of work when I am focusing. My productivity is like the tide at the beach. Sometimes it is roaring, devouring the sands, crashing over the rocks: that is when I am firing on all cylinders, smashing through work, completing projects, coming up with new ideas. And sometimes that tide retreats, ebbing away down the beach to where you can barely see it: this is where I am resting, recovering from the huge amount of effort that has just been put in.

This type of hard work was never shown to me. It was never modelled. And it certainly was never praised. You see, our society respects and rewards only one kind of working hard: putting the time in, day after day, grinding out what needs to be done. This is true of both school and most jobs: for eight hours a day, you must remain focused and on task, doing what needs to be done, like a little machine.

Our society looks at 9-year-old me not going to feed next door's rabbit and says, "She's lazy. She's unreliable. She's not a hard worker." But it doesn't look at 9-year-old me and go, "She's a creative. She's an ideas person." You don't get rewarded for your creativity; you only get judged for your lack of follow-through.

I think it's time to redefine what working hard means for people with ADHD.

- **Old definition of hard work**: consistent, continuous effort, over a long period of time.
- **New definition of hard work**: big bursts of energy in which huge amounts of work are done, alongside a lot of rest.

I think back to 9-year-old me starting Helping Hands. Now I can clearly see the awesome, creative work that I did put in. It is bittersweet to wonder what would have happened if I, and those around me, had known that I had ADHD at the time. Would I have developed differently, if my struggles to complete the job had been viewed as an executive function challenge?

I look at my life now and feel incredibly grateful that I find myself as part of many different teams. Whether it is at home with Rich, writing songs, or designing an app, I have found a place where my ideas and creativity are valued, and where other people with skills in administration, execution and financial planning shine in their own way! So many ADHDers believe that we must do it all. But, no one human should be responsible for doing it all, whether that be running a home, or a business!

The neurodivergent mind will often be the most creative in the room—great at out-of-the-box problem solving, communication, big-picture thinking, and creativity.[4] Those people are valuable and much needed. We must find a way to make space for ourselves within the working world, to allow the way we work to shine through and be supported. Just as those of us with ADHD may need somebody to help finish an idea, the neurotypicals equally might need us to come up with that idea in the first place! We are all very valuable unique cogs in a bigger machine and can complement each other.

ADHDers are many things . . . but lazy isn't one.

Unlearning the "I Am Lazy" Lie

If you have ADHD, it's very likely you will have a deep internalised belief that you are lazy. It will have formed over your lifetime as you collect little pieces of "evidence" to support it: the washing left in the machine, the important work you haven't done, the creative ideas that ran out of steam. It's highly likely you've been called lazy as well, by care-givers, teachers, or in my case, loads of anonymous users on the internet!

Listen up: you are NOT lazy. Rather, you have ADHD, which means you may struggle with certain tasks due to difficulties with executive function. I also know you have the ability to work very hard. You may be incredible with empathy, gifted at creativity, or have a vivid imagination; or maybe you're a wizard at brainstorming or starting a crafts business, or able to spend hours hyperfocusing. These things probably won't feel like hard work to you because they come so easily. But they are extremely valuable skills.

Here are a few tips to kick the lazy lie!

1. **BANISH THE WORD "LAZY"**: The first step is simply to stop calling yourself lazy. Out loud, or internally. If you are struggling to do something, get curious. What's going on? Why is your notivation kicking in? Do you need help? "Lazy" is a word stacked with horrible connotations— you don't need to hear it anymore. The world is still catching up to understanding ADHD, and many people still see us as inherently lazy. It's imperative we show them the truth—that we work really hard in a different way. And that is something to embrace, not judge.

2. **REJECT PRODUCTIVITY CULTURE**: For so many of us, we dream of beating the laziness out of ourselves so we can finally be productive. Finally achieve something. Make people proud of us. And escape that horrible feeling that we are failures. But when this is our goal, we make a catastrophic error! Productivity is not the most important thing in someone's life. There is no moral element to it. Over-focusing on our productivity means we often miss the bigger picture. The real rough diamonds of life: being authentically ourselves, loving people deeply, feeling sorrow and pain, dreaming of better futures, living in safe environments. Our safety and our happiness should be number 1 on our list of priorities. Not our productivity.

3. **REDEFINE "HARD WORK"**: Your definition of what it means to work hard likely needs to change. In a neurotypical world it is very easy to believe that hard work is simply showing up at the same time every day and grinding away on something. Distractions are seen as bad. Rest is seen as unnecessary. But for the ADHD brain, hard work is totally different! It will come in huge bursts of energy and action, followed by much needed rest. It won't follow a tightly defined schedule, but that's the beauty of it. We are colouring outside of the lines of what is expected, and creating our own blueprint for what dedication looks like.

4. **SHARE YOUR REALITY**: Letting loved ones, friends and colleagues know how you work best is an exercise in ADHD advocacy. The more people understand that we don't work well with repetitive daily tasks, but can be absolutely invaluable in a brainstorming meeting, for example, the more the world will start to see the high value of neurodivergent thinkers on a team. It is not selfish to express where your strengths lie, and the right company will relish the opportunity to develop a different kind of talent and perspective. So many of us have hidden our true talents away because we are so overly focused on fixing our perceived flaws.

Reframing the Lie

Instead of this:

~~I am lazy.~~

Try this:

I can sometimes struggle with things others find easy, and that's okay. I work really hard in my own way.

"You're Not Lazy"

Written by Rich

Relationships usually end for a multitude of reasons: unreasonable behaviour, cheating, abuse or incompatibility, to name just a few.

What isn't usually given as a reason is, "I can't handle the clothes all over the bedroom floor." But if Rox and I were ever going to end, this would be why! You see, before her ADHD diagnosis we were caught in what I like to call the "Toxic Tidy Cycle." Here's what that looks like:

1. Rox makes a mess. This could be clothes all over the bedroom floor, a new arts and crafts hyperfocus spread all over the house, or a new superfood smoothie recipe she's found, leading to a trashed kitchen.
2. Rox promises to clean the mess up "later."
3. Rox does not in fact clean the mess up later.
4. I get pretty pissed off, and feel lied to and taken for granted.
5. I end up tidying up, making sure to do it loudly so Rox knows I am pissed off, while quietly letting resentment build.
6. Rox gets defensive and says, "I was gonna do that!"
7. I say, "But you didn't."
8. Both of us feel angry and misunderstood.

Although a messy bedroom doesn't seem like grounds for divorce, the toxic cycle around it brings up some bigger issues. The constant broken promises can really impact trust between two people. The resentment that builds internally can steal your connection and joy. She ends up thinking of me as judgmental. And I end up thinking she's *just lazy*.

But still, angry as I was, the notion that Rox was just lazy was confusing to me. It didn't ring true. I would see her spend all day researching a new hobby, work for hours writing a song, or want to redecorate the spare room at 11 p.m.—and find the energy to do it! The way I saw it, she could be incredibly focused and hard-working when she wanted to be.

Sadly, at first, this led to an even worse thought . . . rather than simply "Rox is lazy." I started to think: "Rox is choosing not to help me."

We were on a one-way road to miscommunication and misunderstanding—and the real possibility of missing out on what has been the most incredible relationship of both of our lives. Now that we have an understanding of ADHD and the challenges faced by people diagnosed with it, our entire conversation around cleaning and tidiness has changed.

The two things I learned about ADHD that had the biggest impact on my ability to lean into understanding Rox, rather than judging her, were:

1. ADHD people often have problems with executive function. Executive function is a cognitive (mental) process that takes care of organizing thoughts and activities, prioritising tasks, and managing time. Many ADHD people will therefore struggle to organize and stick with tasks. Like cleaning.[5]

2. ADHDers have an "interest-based" nervous system. This means it seeks high-stimulation situations, stronger incentives, and more immediate rewards. These in turn trigger a quick and intense release of dopamine and a rush of motivation.[6] Let me be clear: cleaning clothes up off the floor does not stimulate the dopamine injection that Rox will be craving.

What this meant was game-changing for our relationship dynamic. *She wasn't doing it on purpose. She wasn't being lazy.* You see, the clothes on the floor weren't really the problem. Yes, a clean house is lovely, but the mess triggered negative thoughts in me because it was touching on something a lot deeper: the feeling that my needs didn't matter, and that my partner was purposefully choosing to not help me around the house.

It's very easy to judge somebody's actions—or inaction—and have no idea what is actually going on underneath. Of course, the best way to know how somebody is feeling is simply to ask. This was something I had never done with Rox until this point. If she promised to do something and didn't do it, I assumed it was intentional. The first time I addressed things directly with her, everything shifted.

"Babe," I began, "you promised you would clean the bedroom today. I'm finding it a bit difficult that you haven't done it. I'd really like to know what's going on for you."

"Honestly, I have no idea," Rox said. "I am so, so sorry I am affecting you. When I promised to do it, I really, truly believed I would. It's like I never learn my words mean nothing. I honestly think I am just really lazy."

Hearing this triggered massive amounts of compassion in me. Here was this person that I deeply love, twisted in knots because she was struggling to do something that is considered basic, feeling guilty because it was affecting me, and choosing to label herself in a really negative way. Suddenly I could see I had been reflecting back to her what her core negative belief was! And when someone believes deeply that they are lazy, they won't ask for help, and they won't be able to imagine things getting better.

But things do get better. In our case, we replaced our Toxic Tidy Cycle with something that actually works. Behold, our Wonky Tidy Cycle:

1. Rox makes a mess.
2. Rox promises to tidy it up later.
3. I kindly remind her that it's now or never with her, and ask if there's anything I can do to help her get started.
4. Rox will often ask me to sit with her while she works, or to break the tasks into steps and advise her where to start.
5. The mess is cleaned and we both feel better!

The simple offer of help can often be the little injection of dopamine needed to get an ADHDer started on a task. And let me be clear about something: I have been accused on the internet of doing everything for Rox. That simply isn't true. And in fact, doing everything for someone with ADHD can do as much harm as criticising them. In Rox's case, it means she wouldn't start to build a new core belief that she is actually way more capable than she ever believed.

My offering to assist Rox is about creating an environment of kindness and encouragement so that she can help me with tasks around the house and we can both feel a sense of pride over our work. We don't simply replace the core belief of "I am lazy" with "I can't do it, so others always have to do it for me." Rather, we want to replace it with "I can do it if I have the right support."

So, to sum up, we won't be petitioning the government to add "Clothes all over the floor" as legal grounds for divorce any time soon . . . which is great news.

How to Help an ADHDer Who Believes They're Lazy

Your ADHDer likely has a lifetime of hearing "You're so lazy!" from parents, teachers and colleagues. They may also have heard it from you. This doesn't make you a bad person. But once we know better, we can do better.

Here are a few suggestions to help flip the script and replace the toxic core belief with new, more helpful messages:

1. **FIND THE REAL STORY**: Rather than drawing your own conclusions about why your ADHDer is not doing something, **get curious**. Ask what is going on for them. Often you will hear that they are overwhelmed, or that they are confused about how to get started on a task. The real story will inspire compassion in you, rather than judgment (as in my example of my conversation with Rox, above). And compassion is a much better starting point for action. Your ADHDer will understandably be used to lying, defending themselves, and covering up their struggles. So, it will take practice, patience and trust-building to get to a place where they feel safe enough to share what is really going on.

2. **HELP UNLOCK NOTIVATION**: Often, a stumbling block for a low-dopamine task is just getting started. Your ADHDer might be confused about what the first step is, or may feel too overwhelmed to begin. As I mentioned, you don't want to do the task for them: it's important they begin to build self-esteem by doing it themselves! But offering to help or by advising on which step to take first—can really make a difference. Body-doubling has been a *huge* help in our house! This is when an ADHD person has a task to

complete, and you sit with them. You don't even need to do anything! Just the act of doubling them (being in the room with them) helps them to take action.

3. **USE DOPAMINE HACKS**: After years of living with Rox, I have figured out a few little hacks which always seem to get her working. I sort of hope she doesn't read this and figure out what I've been up to! But . . . this is too good not to share. We know that ADHD brains are lacking in dopamine, which is often why tasks can be difficult to start. So I will set little dopamine rewards at the end of a chunk of manageable work. For example . . . "Babe, after we've finished work today shall we go to the cinema?" or "I'm going to go and get us some chocolate when we've done our work." Even offering to run a hot bath with scented candles can be enough of a motivator for her to get started. Sprinkling in little bits of dopamine throughout the day when milestones are reached is a game-changer!

4. **BANISH THE WORD "LAZY"**: I can't stress this step enough. If you hear your ADHDer calling themselves lazy, reflect back to them all of the ways you see them working really hard. This might be on a creative project, planning a dream, or a new hyperfocus. We want to reinforce that they work hard in their own way. If I see Rox working on a new song idea, or re-arranging the bedroom, or painting a jacket on the kitchen table, I'll make a point of saying I've noticed how hard she has been working. Their passions and hobbies have often been shamed, and they have been made to feel like the only work that matters is a more neurotypical way of doing things . . . Every person in a family, relationship or company has unique strengths to bring. Allowing different strengths to be celebrated creates a shame-free and diverse environment where everybody can thrive.

Reframing the Lie

When they say this:

~~I am lazy.~~

Try telling them this:

You work really hard in your own way.

You are a lot more capable than the world has made you believe.

ADHD Lie #2: I'm Not Trying Hard Enough

Written by Rox

I was 34 years old when I made the first decision that would untangle the train wreck that was my life. That decision was to get sober. The car-crash breakups, the mounting debt, the secret self-harm . . . It had all gotten to be too much. My daily alcohol intake had left me looking bloated and aged beyond my years; I was having blackouts most evenings.

Most addicts have a moment of "rock bottom"—that one event that tells you, loud and clear, that you simply cannot continue to live as you have been. My rock bottom happened in Ibiza, a Spanish island with a reputation for hardcore partying. To cut a long and shameful story short, I missed a video shoot for work. I cheated on my partner. And I stayed awake for three days. When I arrived home, I knew I couldn't go on hurting people, and myself, in this way. Not long after that, I walked into my first recovery meeting, and I am beyond grateful to say that, as I write this, I have celebrated five years sober. When I say sobriety saved my life, I mean it with everything inside me. My life was heading in an extremely dangerous direction, the outcomes of which would have been jail or death.

People with ADHD are five to ten times more likely to struggle with alcohol addiction.[7] In some ways, this is not surprising: alcohol is a depressant, meaning it can have a calming effect on hyperactivity. For me, drinking helped to quiet the racing thoughts in my mind and to dial back my almost constant anxiety. Three drinks in and I felt normal for the night. I felt present. But the harsh reality is that I was self-medicating ADHD and trauma with alcohol without even knowing it. I suspect many undiagnosed neurodivergents are living the same hellish cycle that I was.

As with most newly sober people, I was overcome with a huge desire to change myself for the better. To wipe my slate clean and begin again. I wanted all of my unsavoury behaviour gone. So, along with quitting the day-drinking and promiscuity, I decided it was time to *focus*. Oh dear . . . I find myself shaking my head at 34-year-old me. Feeling so sorry for her—the undiagnosed ADHDer deciding it was finally time to "get organized."

However, I did manage to make a lot of changes in my first year of recovery. Here are the lifelong habits that I managed to change:

- I stayed off alcohol.
- I stayed off drugs.
- I went celibate.

Before I got sober, alcohol was my best friend. My favourite part of any day. I had pictures of pints of beer on my Instagram feed. I was always first at the bar and last to leave. And I didn't need to be in a bar to drink. I drank every evening until I couldn't string a sentence together. I would go to weddings purely for the open bar. I'd leave work events slurring, and usually with someone I shouldn't be with. My fridge was always stocked with champagne and beer. And if I ran out, I knew the location of every corner shop that was open late for alcohol within a five-mile radius.

Sex and relationships were another obsession of mine. I hadn't been single since I was 16. My relationships were extremely intense, short-lived and overlapping. I often had multiple love interests going on while I was in long-term relationships. I moved in with every partner early on, believing every time that it would last forever. Falling in lust was intoxicating to me. The less available the person was emotionally, the deeper I would fall. I was obsessed with finding the love of my life, and I pursued that fantasy as if my life depended on it. When the excitement of a new relationship would end, I would begin the hunt for that hit of emotions from somebody else. I simply could not be on my own: I needed the high of somebody else to function.

So, when I tell you that I managed to quit both the booze and the relationships, I hope you understand that I had to try *extremely hard* to do that. Regular recovery meetings, deep personal work, brutal accountability, strong willpower—and an obsessive consumption of self-help books and podcasts. It took every ounce of strength in me not to go back to my old habits. For me, it was miraculous. I had never imagined I could achieve something like this. And that gruelling experience taught me that if a person tried hard enough, they could change anything.

So, compared to beating my alcohol and sex addiction, getting organized and keeping my space clean would be a walk in the park, right?

I bought every book there was on productivity and habit forming. I would consume each one avidly, and implement the new strategies with military precision. My life would change for a couple of weeks (at best), and I would feel on top of the world. Fixed. Better. Trying hard. And then . . . like clockwork, I would fail. And each failure left me feeling even worse than before. How, I asked myself, could I quit alcohol and sex, but not quit being disorganized?!

And once again, I totally ignored the other factors at play:

- I never acknowledged the hard work I had put into my sobriety.
- I never wondered if something else might be going on.

Instead, I simply screamed at myself that I wasn't trying hard enough, and tried again. And again. And again. You've got to hand it to us neurodivergents: we have been trying and failing to get organized for years, but we still hold onto the delusion that it's possible to simply *will* ourselves to improve.

It was self-improvement Groundhog Day. Trying over and over again. Always falling short. My room was a mess. My laundry wasn't done. I had 32,198 unread emails. I wasn't sticking to my eight-hours-a-day work schedule—and I didn't understand what was wrong with me.

How could I beat addiction, but not manage to take my coffee cup downstairs?! What the hell was happening?

A couple of years later, when my journey led me to seek an ADHD diagnosis, I began to look at my many failed attempts at fixing certain parts of myself. The truth was laid out before me. My problems were:

- Symptoms of a neurodevelopmental condition.
- Not a personal failure.

I want to say this louder for the people in the back still gaslighting themselves that they just need to try harder. My problems were:

- Symptoms of a neurodevelopmental condition.
- Not a personal failure.

Even though it rang completely true, it still felt like the easy way out. It felt like riding the coattails of some trendy diagnosis, rather than taking responsibility for what a truly awful person I was. My internalised self-hatred (hello, voice of the critical parent . . .) was loud. Incredibly, even after struggling so hard my whole life with things other people could do in their sleep, I still felt the need to be punished. Self-compassion felt like coddling. Like excuses.

There's real grief in that. If you have truly believed your whole life that somewhere out there is a version of you that is great with time, organized and calm, then accepting a diagnosis of ADHD is like letting go of that fantasy that was always your reason for trying. "Who am I if I'm not trying to be normal?" I asked myself. I had a deep fear that if I stopped my desperate attempt to fix myself, everything would unravel. The little bit of control I did have, thanks to my constant masking (hiding of symptoms) and anxiety, would give way to absolute chaos.

Eventually, I learned that the total opposite was true. It was the acceptance of ADHD that enabled me to actually "fix" what was wrong with me. You see, I'd been working on the wrong things. It wasn't my time-keeping or my problems with memory or organization that were "broken." It was how I spoke to myself, how I hated myself. That's what the problem was. Diagnosis meant that I could finally stop trying to overcome symptoms with willpower. It meant I could learn to accept there were always going to be things I struggled with. And it meant I could learn to love that person, just as she is.

I want to be clear about something here: working to better yourself is a remarkable act. Getting sober and going to therapy were difficult, yet ultimately life-saving decisions—ones that have made me happier, healthier, and probably a lot nicer to be around! Healing journeys are the deep work of a lifetime that allow us to become emotionally and spiritually mature. I believe wholeheartedly in learning, and deepening our connection to ourselves, our communities and our world. But I also believe that we cannot learn ourselves out of a mental condition. Willpower and "trying harder" will simply not magic away the ADHD.

If you have ADHD, you are forever trying to achieve something you weren't born for. Something physically impossible. Believing that if you stick to the task long enough, try hard enough, you will eventually beat your symptoms into submission. However, what you really need is to understand and accept who you are, and then begin to create ways to support your needs.

My chosen family—Rich, Seer and Lillie (my two stepchildren)—have helped me to do exactly that. In our home, I get to live out loud. Warts and all. They accept that I am messy, forgetful, unorganized. And also highly creative, deeply empathetic, and a keen problem solver. But most importantly? I am loved deeply, and valued. My symptoms aren't ignored, belittled or judged. I don't feel I need to fix them, or myself. I get to exist just as I am, and to be supported in the places that I need it.

Had I not decided to accept who I was, this book wouldn't exist. "Fixing" myself was a full-time job. Instead of writing, I would no doubt have been implementing some new system on how to stop losing things, or devising a plan for how to keep a super-tidy sock drawer.

Think about your own situation: What would happen if you took all of that 'try harder' energy and put it towards something you really care about? Something you're naturally good at, that truly feels like it makes you alive?

Trying harder to beat ADHD symptoms is like banging your head against a brick wall. Spending that energy on projects that you love, though, just might change your life. Perhaps your life's purpose isn't having the cleanest house in town. Perhaps it is something else . . . something way better!

So here's a new mantra:

"I just need to try harder *to accept myself as I am.*"

The fact we have been trying and failing for so long to outsmart ADHD will have left so many of us hopeless. The reason you haven't made any progress is that you have been trying to change something that cannot be changed! But there are many things in this life we can change . . . for me it was getting sober, getting therapy, having my first healthy relationship, and finding career success in my thirties. I wonder what it is for you?

Unlearning the "I'm Not Trying Hard Enough" Lie

Think about how long you have been forcing yourself to try harder, each time coming up against the same old problems, over and over again. I truly want you to reflect on this, although it may be painful: how has forcing yourself to try harder worked out for you? Are you happier? Are you more fulfilled? Are you no longer experiencing ADHD symptoms?

Next, I want you to internalise what I am about to say. Highlight it. Write it down. Get it tattooed. Do whatever you need to do so you can come to terms with this, over and over again.

You cannot stop ADHD symptoms by trying harder. In fact, the added pressure will often make those symptoms worse. The only things that help are acceptance and support.

I understand the fear this brings up. The self-gaslighting. The worry that if you let yourself off the hook, things will fall apart. But I promise you that will not happen. Somebody who is short-sighted does not need to try harder to see the sign 20 metres away. They need glasses. In the same way, somebody with ADHD doesn't need to try harder to overcome their very real symptoms. They need understanding and help.

Here are a few key ways to go about this:

1. **ACCEPT THAT YOU HAVE ADHD**: It isn't a "get out of jail free" card. It isn't an excuse. It is a very real medical condition that affects focus, working memory, organization, administrational tasks, time-keeping, impulsivity, and so much more. Please stop denying yourself compassion and support. Trying harder simply leads to frustration, and is a one-way street to burnout. You have ADHD. That means you are going to struggle with some things others find easy. There is no shame in that.

2. **TRY HARD AT SOMETHING ELSE**: Hard work will always bring about results, if you find the right thing to work on. Going to the gym every day will build muscle and fitness. Writing 200 words a day will lead to writing a book. Therapy every week will lead to a better understanding of yourself. There are so many incredible things you can achieve by trying harder, but sometimes when we have spent years trying and failing to fix a condition, we can lose faith in our ability to shift things in our life: to bring dreams

to fruition, or to make massive change. The only reason you have lost faith is that you have been trying to change a constant, not a variable. Take all of that time and energy and apply it somewhere else. You will be astounded by the results.

3. **STOP TRYING TO FIX WHAT ISN'T BROKEN**: The reason so many of us get caught in the "must try harder" loop is that we truly believe we aren't okay. That we aren't valuable just as we are. What would life look like if you stopped believing you needed fixing, and instead fixed your environment, your self-talk, and your view of yourself? We can become so obsessed with fixing what we see as personal failings that we never try to fix things we can actually change. There is a beautiful prayer I learned in recovery that goes like this: *God, grant me the serenity to accept the things I cannot change. The courage to change the things I can. And the wisdom to know the difference.* You cannot change your ADHD symptoms. But you absolutely can manage them with the right knowledge and support.

4. **KEEP KIND COMPANY**: Cultivate a chosen group of people who see your value. Who love you. Who know you aren't doing things on purpose. And who know you are trying your best. You absolutely do not need to stay in places that reflect back your inner belief that you are somehow unworthy of love because you have a mental health condition. Nobody gets to tell you to try harder. If you have to associate with people who assume the worst about you, set boundaries with them.

Reframing the Lie

Instead of this:

~~I'm not trying hard enough.~~

Try this:
I am trying my best.
I don't need to "fix" myself.

"You're Doing Your Best"

Written by Rich

Here's my morning routine if I'm going out:

1. It actually begins the night before with Googling travel plans. This helps me determine the time I need to leave.
2. On the morning of my appointment or event, my alarm goes off with time to spare (and a couple of snoozes factored in).
3. I get up and mainline some coffee.
4. I have a shower and get dressed.
5. I leave for my appointment, usually with a decent amount of spare time. This helps ensure that I'm neither late (nor ridiculously early) unless something incredibly unusual happens that's beyond my control.

Here's Rox's morning routine:

1. She wakes up.

2. She sometimes checks her calendar to see if she has something on. (Occasionally, she forgets this step and will receive a text saying "Where are you?" from whoever was expecting her.)

3. She checks how long it will take her to get to where she is going and decides what time she needs to leave the house to get there right on the dot. She allows herself zero wiggle room.

4. She wildly underestimates how long it will actually take her to get ready, believing she can get ready in ten minutes rather than the usual thirty minutes.

5. Fifteen minutes before she's due to leave, her outfit will start feeling scratchy. She gets overstimulated and needs to change clothes.

6. The situation now becomes highly stressful, as she's rushing around late.

7. She won't be able to find her wallet / phone / keys / sunglasses etc., and the panic will increase. Now her face is probably flushed and sweaty.

8. She'll finally have everything ready, but will miss the train she had planned to get.

9. She'll have to shamefully text someone to say she is running late once again.

This happens every single time she has somewhere to be. And she believes with 100 percent conviction that her timings and planning will work. Every time they don't, she is genuinely confused by how this could have happened, and that confusion is often accompanied by panicking and tears.

In the beginning of our relationship, this behaviour didn't make sense to me. How could somebody make the same mistakes over and over and over again and never learn? I gave her advice about planning her journeys the night before, laying out outfits, and leaving wiggle room for journey times. Each time, her behaviours would improve for a week or so before reverting back.

The result for me was that every morning, through no fault of my own, I was having to be engaged in a stressful environment. A mad search for sunglasses, a quick drive to the train station, lending my headphones . . . Rox could feel my frustration. And when she was finally on a train to where she was going, I'd get a text that read like this:

Hi Bubby, I'm so sorry I was running late this morning. It must be so stressful. I promise you I'll try harder. Love you, Rox xx

I know without any doubt she meant those words deeply. But the evidence I had in front of me was that, no matter how hard she said she was trying, nothing was actually going to change. That was a pretty confusing situation. And I was faced with two explanations:

1. She was lying. She wasn't trying at all, and she was disrupting my mornings on purpose.
2. She really was trying her best, but for whatever reason, that wasn't working.

It would have been so easy for me to go with explanation 1. It was the only one that made sense to me, based on my brain wiring, and how I work. It was inconceivable to me that such a chaotic situation actually *was* Rox's best, at that moment.

I want partners and parents of ADHDers to understand that you are not a bad person for getting frustrated. And for not understanding. It took me a lot of time and effort—challenging my own thinking, reading books, speaking to a therapist, and truly learning about ADHD—before

I understood what was truly going on and Rox and I were able to find a really happy place. A place where I know Rox is always trying her best.

An ADHD diagnosis can be really hard to comprehend at first, and I think the main reason is that we cannot *see* ADHD. It's not immediately visible to other people, the way a cast on a broken leg tells you a person is not going to be running a marathon any time soon, or the way diabetes shows up in a series of medical tests. ADHD is what's known as a hidden or invisible disability. Just because you can't see someone's limitations, doesn't mean they're not there.

Before Rox's diagnosis, I spent so much time wishing she would change. Wishing she would be on time, be less clumsy, and not always leave in a panic. I can tell you now, though, that was all wasted time. Trying to force someone to change who they are at their core is only going to hurt both people. Looking at Rox through an ADHD lens, I was finally able to see someone who was having anxiety attacks most mornings. Nobody would choose that—letting people down at work. Spending extra time travelling due to missed trains. And what made it sadder is that Rox herself truly believed that if she just tried harder, she would change. But Rox had been trying to change for almost four decades.

It wasn't just the morning routine that Rox had been hopelessly trying to improve. The "just try harder" effect hit many areas of her life:

- **ORGANIZATION**: new notebooks, endless to-do lists, every ADHD app going
- **TIDINESS**: countless attempts to keep clothes off the "floordrobe" (our word for clothing scattered on the floor) and take coffee cups downstairs
- **COMMUNICATION**: promises to do better at texting back friends and family

- **TIME MANAGEMENT**: setting alarms, creating reminders, making promises to stop being late

And none of it had ever worked.

Even now, it still makes me sad to read this list. No matter what Rox tried, no matter how hard she worked or how earnest her intentions, it never actually helped at all. She still had ADHD. That list symbolises her total rejection of who she was, in an attempt to be neurotypical.

After we began to understand ADHD, we accepted that the work we needed to do together wasn't about making her try harder: it was about helping her—and me—accept who she was.

One key change that we made significantly altered a negative core belief we both held. It's no longer about Rox needing to try harder; it's about her (and me) understanding she's trying her best. You can't be angry or upset with someone who is genuinely trying their best. This lens swap is critical in ADHD households.

Switch "You need to try harder" to "I see you're trying your best."

The first message is judgmental; the second is validating and kind.

Trying to change who you are at your core is an impossible task. It's also highly stressful. And trust me, when you have ADHD, life is stressful enough.

So . . . going back to our morning routine, here's how it looks now. I'll happily be there to help Rox search for wallets, look at train times, and provide much-needed "regulation cuddles." (A regulation cuddle is where you use body contact—a cuddle—to help someone calm their nervous system.)

When you treat your ADHDer as someone who is trying their best, and as someone who is valuable no matter what they are struggling with, they will feel safe to unmask, to show their real self. What this actually looks like in our household is Rox asking for help, or crying if she is overwhelmed, or asking for something specific. The internal battles she tried to hide for so long now have a safe place to come out and be dealt with together. Many ADHDers have had a lifetime of pretending to be okay, of holding in their panic, their tears, and frustration. Creating a safe and calm emotional space at home is the best way to help them drop the years of believing that their problems are their fault, and to show them that they are not alone with what they are dealing with.

Now the texts I get from Rox after a mad dash to the train station aren't apologies and desperate promises that she will try harder. They are thank-yous. When your ADHDer is thanking you for your help and support, rather than constantly apologising (which is sometimes referred to as "fawning"), that is when you have struck spicy house gold.

How to Help an ADHDer Who Believes They're Not Trying Hard Enough

Your ADHDer will likely have a loud internal bully screaming at them, telling them that if they just tried harder, their struggles would stop. They are living in a constant state of anxiety, desperately trying, and failing, at self-improvement. This leads to incredibly low self-esteem.

It's imperative to help them understand that no matter how hard they try, they won't cure their ADHD symptoms. And that's okay.

Instead, aim for providing an environment where they can be honest about their struggles. And the new standard will be that trying their best is all that is needed.

Here are a few suggestions on how to create that new, kinder environment:

1. **KINDLY CALL OUT THE BULLSHIT**: ADHDers believe that trying harder will fix their symptoms. This isn't the case. It never has been. And it never will be. Kindly reminding them that promises to try harder and get better will only lead to disappointment for both of you. Help them understand that trying their best is all they can do. For example: texting a friend and saying "I'm so sorry I ignored your message. I will make sure that this never happens again" is a false promise. The ADHDer truly believes it in the moment, but this kind of promise sets them up to fail. It's better to be honest than promise yourself into a prison.

2. **PROVIDE VALIDATION**: Your ADHDer has likely heard a great deal of negative feedback over their lifetime, and will have internalised a negative core view of themselves leading to a desperate desire to change. Telling them you see them trying their best and that you are proud of them is vitally important to help reverse this narrative. Look for areas where they are especially hard on themselves; for example, losing things, or cleaning. Those are the areas where we need to acknowledge that we see the incredible effort they are making.

3. **HELP WHERE YOU CAN**: Body-doubling with your ADHDer, where you sit with them as they tackle a difficult task, will accomplish much more than shaming them. Helping them find their phone when it's lost will be way more helpful than simply telling them not to lose it. We have to fully accept that ADHD causes symptoms beyond this person's control and be there to support them when they need it. Stifle the urge to tell them how to change or get angry at them for an honest mistake. If you can help, why not do it?

4. **CHANNEL CALMNESS**: A huge part of ADHD is emotional dysregulation. This may be brought on by losing something, running late, perceived criticism, and many other things. Being a calm and stable nervous system for your ADHDer will provide them with the safety and regulation they need. So often with Rox, when she's in a panic, all I need to do is wrap my arms around her. She might have a cry, or take some deep breaths. And then she feels infinitely better.

Reframing the Lie

When they say this:

I'm not trying hard enough.

Try telling them this:
You are trying your best.
You don't have to do this alone.

ADHD Lie #3: I Quit Everything I Start

Written by Rox

Common wisdom says that to become an expert in something, you need 10,000 hours of dedicated practice. I would like to put it to you that I am a world-renowned expert on quitting. If there is one area of this book where my expertise will truly shine, it is this one. I don't mean to be arrogant, but I do want you to know that you are learning from a true expert on this subject. So, if you don't mind, I'd like to share with you just a few of my many credentials:

Rox's quitting experience:

- 23 jobs
- 10 relationships
- 89 creative pursuits
- The second season of *The Walking Dead*
- 100 percent of the countless diets I have ever started
- 100 percent of the attempts to be organized I have ever tried

A quote from a former employer:

Her ability to quit after three months of starting the job was like nothing we had ever seen. No notice. No real explanation. Just a text message sent on a Friday evening and she never came back in again. If you are looking for a quitter to join your team, you could not find someone better than Roxanne.

Personal reference:

My daughter has quit everything from a young age. Her piano lessons. Her dreams of going to Oxford University. And then pretty much every poor sod she happened to be in a relationship with and every job she has ever sworn was her next life's purpose. I am constantly amazed by her quitting ability.

My record is untarnished. I am qualified—I have a PhD in quitting. In fact, I could give a TED Talk on quitting. The audience would be hanging on my every word as I imparted my wisdom to them. It would sound something like this:

. . . you wait for the perfect moment. When all the stars are aligned. When you truly feel you are on to something very special. When everybody around you is finally starting to believe a miracle has occurred and this new life purpose is going to be the one that will actually stick. When you have announced your plans to all of your friends and family with extreme confidence. When you have spent an inordinate amount of money on making your dreams a reality. When you are ready to seriously take things to the next level and finally achieve your potential. BOOM. That's when you quit. Leaving all of that potential still on the table. Leaving your dreams to die. It's perfect . . . Everyone was sort of expecting it, but your incredible confidence had them fooled yet again. That is how you quit.

Truthfully, if I didn't laugh, I'd cry. Quitting comes with so much shame. And a lot of confusion. Every time I start something, I have this utterly naive belief that it will be different this time. Through one lens it can be seen as an act of insanity, as Albert Einstein put it: insanity is doing the same thing over and over again and expecting a different result. Through another lens, it's a sign of incredible resilience: dreaming of a better future over and over again, despite all the evidence to the contrary.

I began developing my skills as a quitter at a really young age. From my short-lived business venture at 9 years old, to my decision to stop learning the piano at Grade 7 (there are only eight grades). I found myself ducking out of things at the most inopportune times, and to the annoyance of people around me. But it wasn't until I quit my first post-graduate job that I really cemented my status as a champion quitter. That's when I joined the big leagues.

In life, there is an often-mysterious set of neurotypical rules and expectations governing all of our behaviour. Nobody ever tells you these rules, explains them to you, or even questions whether they might be right for you. They are just ... there. You must intuit them from observing how your successful friends choose to live, and where the general direction of a well-lived life seems to be flowing. And whatever you do ... do not deviate from this unwritten path. If you do, you run the risk of looking like a quitter, a lazy person or a loser.

The unwritten neurotypical rules for success (that nobody ever taught you):

1. Allow an interest to develop in your teenage years.
2. Study this interest at college and possibly university.
3. Get your first job within this area of interest.
4. Work your way up through the ranks.
5. Retire at 65 and be given a gold watch and a card signed by the entire office.

And I tried my best to follow these rules. I went to university, and ended up getting a graduate job at an accountancy firm. I couldn't have picked a more ill-fitting job if I tried! But this was the expected path, and I followed it as best I could.

Quitting my accountancy training after three months was a momentous and shame-filled decision for me. I felt like I was letting my entire family down, and squandering an amazing opportunity. I stuck it out as long as I possibly could, but in December 2006 my mum died after a three-year battle with cancer and, strangely enough, that was the catalyst that allowed me to quit the job. I finally felt like I had a reason to leave, one that had nothing to do with me just being a quitter. I had a reason people would have to be kind about, and would have to understand. Simply saying I was deeply uncomfortable and struggling with the work was an unacceptable reason to me.

I knew, however, that I needed another job ASAP. One I was going to stick at for the rest of my life.

So off I went to apply for other jobs. At the same time, I was struggling with desperate grief over my mum's death, and had absolutely zero support. I felt utterly hopeless and lost without her. She was the one person who had looked at me kindly and treated me with love no matter how much I was failing at basic tasks. But I had become so accustomed to acting like I was okay, to pretending I had things under control, that I never told anybody how difficult I was finding life without her. I didn't have the language to tell my dad or anyone else how much pain I was in.

We never spoke about emotions in my house growing up. We swept difficult things under the rug, swallowed down the pain, and went on as normal. Affairs, abuse, cancer. The bigger the topic, the less likely my family was to speak about it. Given this, I was unable to ask for the help I so desperately craved after my mum passed. My dad moved on in his own way, marrying another woman whom I had known about for a long time. My family home became their home. My bedroom became her dressing room. Strange how such a small action, like redecorating a room, can leave such deep scars. I suppose the message I took was that I was no longer welcome, and that I didn't matter. My dad of course deserved happiness, and company. It just makes me sad that it often came at my expense. I sometimes wonder if things might have been different if I'd had the language to tell him how lost I was.

And my friends didn't know either. One of my closest friends recently sent me a long apology about not being there when my mum died. She explained that she truly didn't know how much I was suffering. I bear absolutely no ill will towards her, or any of my friends, for not knowing. When you have masked your struggles for your entire life, you get pretty good at it. People see the happy, hyper exterior, and have no idea how lonely you are inside.

Numbing the grief with equal parts alcohol and avoidance, I set about finding a new job. One I would stick to this time. Applying for new jobs is a perfect breeding ground for hyperfocus. New mini challenges to obsess over and win. It will come as no surprise to you that my decision to find my forever job did not in fact work out; that in the years that followed, I would apply for, get and quit many jobs in my desperate search to find somewhere I belonged.

It turned out I was great at getting jobs, but not so great at sticking with them. Throughout my twenties I held down the following positions:

- Beauty editor's assistant at a high-end fashion magazine
- Event coordinator at a cancer charity
- Team assistant at a hedge fund
- Singer-songwriter
- Trainee sales-trader at an investment bank

- Barmaid at a pub
- Record label assistant
- Artist manager
- Graphic designer

Each of these jobs lasted anywhere from a few weeks to a couple of years. But I was never happy. My life was coloured by instability. Every job change hit me with the horrifying thought that I was starting again at step 1. Every new job I got was an entry-level position, whereas friends of mine were already receiving their first promotions in their chosen careers. As the years went on, I fell further and further behind where I was meant to be. Further away from benchmarks of neurotypical success. I'd like another Facebook post about someone else's promotion as I headed off for my shift at the pub.

Every new job that I thought was the answer lit up my brain like a little dopamine-fuelled fireworks display, but after a while every single one weighed me down further.

What was really going on?

I only recently learned about the ADHD cycle of interest, and how my job-hopping was actually very common for neurodivergent people. It wasn't in fact evidence of me being a hopeless human; rather, it made total sense given how my brain functioned. How my interests and passions developed and changed. For the first time, I looked back at my mammoth collection of "failed" jobs and saw what was really happening: a person with undiagnosed ADHD trying their best to find a career.

Let me share with you the cycle of interest, in the hopes it may have a similar shame-busting effect on you:

The ADHD 'Cycle of Interest'

1. Discover something new that feels like our life purpose
2. Hyperfocus on it and make it a job
3. Believe this is the best thing ever
4. Lose the love for it
5. Feel hopeless and unmotivated
6. Quit
7. Feel unrelenting shame
8. Begin the cycle again

The way I had always understood success—a straight line from teenage interest to lifelong career—is totally at odds with how the ADHD mind works. The ADHD mind is built for novelty. No wonder my first few weeks in a new job always felt so exciting! And no wonder that, after some time, it would feel like torture. I was working against myself without even knowing it. Trying to force myself yet again into round holes, when I was a square peg.

So let me bring you to my current-day reality. I have a job as a singer/songwriter, one that I love and that would pay me fairly decently if I didn't spend all the money I earn on music videos. I also make ADHD educational content on the internet, and I am in the process of writing my second book (if you're reading this . . . I did it!). To the outside eye I look like I am living a fairly successful life, a far cry from the sofa-surfing and crippling debt of just five years ago. I absolutely love my jobs, and have found stability both financially and romantically.

Finding out I had ADHD was the starting point to reassessing my entire life and the expectations I put on myself. Suddenly the kid who quit everything became a young person with a novelty-seeking brain, doing what they were programmed to do. I slowly let go of the shame and the weight of not meeting neurotypical standards and began the wonderful and difficult process of creating a life for myself that fitted the way I work.

Trying to adopt neurotypical behaviour when you have an ADHD brain is incredibly uncomfortable. It's time to write our own rules. To re-invent a definition of success that is open to us, and that supports the way that we are wired. A place where novelty is valued. Where changing paths isn't shamed. And where the way our brains work is celebrated.

Let me be clear for user890765444, who will undoubtedly comment "So you're saying it's just okay to quit everything, never try hard at anything, and never achieve?"

My response would be this: of course not! Sticking at things is really important. Resilience and hard work are amazing skills! But knowing yourself deeply and knowing when it is time to walk away from something, or someone, is equally valid. We learn so much about what isn't right for us that we get closer to what is.

I wouldn't have found the happiness I now have in my life, had I not quit the million things that weren't quite right that came before. I now see quitting as a really brave thing to do! In the face of pressure from the outside world, and the neurotypical rules, to stand up and say "no thank you" when something doesn't make us happy is such a beautiful and necessary act for many of us. Some people fall into a job, or relationship, that they absolutely love early on in life. Good for them! Some of us need to fail and quit our way into what works for us.

That being said, we also need protection from some of our most impulsive thoughts and behaviours as well . . . The biggest difference for me in healing my deep belief that I was a "quitter" was not actually to stop quitting. Rather, it was to stop *starting* so many things. That is the number 1 life-changing hack I can share with you as a world-renowned quitter: Don't start. I'm not saying don't start *anything*, but I am saying be considerate, careful and thoughtful about what you do start. I have zero of those qualities, by the way, but luckily for me, my wonderful partner has them in spades and helps me to apply that focus.

With ADHD, achievement can look really different. It isn't about a straight line upwards in one direction. It's a million little rollercoasters taking you all over the place. One may take you to a life's purpose; another may take you to a two-day hyperfocus. Who knows? There are lessons to learn and achievements to unlock with every new interest that is pursued.

Many great businesses, inventions or love stories began with a human being with a wild dream. Someone who had to try, and fail, many times before finding their place. So, here's to the quitters. The ones who are brave enough to say "no, thank you" when something doesn't feel good and look for something better.

Unlearning the "I Quit Everything I Start" Lie

If you have ADHD, it's likely that you have had more jobs and more interests than most people. Unfortunately, this can come with a lot of shame. An unwritten rule of society is that quitting is bad—so when we stack up the number of projects we've left behind, we can begin to feel like failures. "Why can't I just stick to one thing?!" becomes yet another stick we beat ourselves over the head with.

Here's a different take: often, quitting is a necessary path to success. Carrying the shame of quitting will have us burned out in jobs we hate, or not taking chances on a new idea that may just be the thing we have been looking for all along.

Here are a few things to keep in mind:

1. **QUITTING CAN BE GOOD**: There is no moral value in forcing yourself to spend the majority of your life doing something you don't enjoy. There's no medal at the end of it. If you are desperately unhappy with your job, there is no shame in looking into other opportunities. Forcing yourself to stay because you feel you may be judged for quitting is forcing yourself to live up to societal rules that are not made for you. Let go of the shame of changing directions, and get really interested in something that's a great fit for you.

2. **HAVE FUN WITHOUT THE PRESSURE**: Your brain is wired to enjoy novelty. Don't deny it something that makes it feel amazing just because it doesn't fit the world's view of "success." You do not have to monetise every hobby, and you do not have to stick with hobbies for the long term. Learn to: make soap, resin, build websites, write a song, host a podcast—go wherever your heart takes you. Allow yourself to enjoy the process of discovering and learning new skills without any further commitment. You may discover something that could become a lifelong career, or perhaps a two-year journey, or even just the hyperfocus of an afternoon. Allow yourself the flexibility to pursue your interests, with no more rules and regulations.

3. **REMEMBER—IT'S A NEUROTYPICAL
   WORLD**: Success is seen as achieving a number of
   milestones at set times over a lifetime. Studying to get a
   degree, getting a job, a promotion and a pension. It's a
   straight line to a final destination. But often that is not the
   path to success for ADHDers. There is no shame in
   walking a different path; in fact, it is something to be proud
   of. May you walk confidently in the direction of your
   dreams, wherever they may take you.

4. **IMAGINATION IS MAGICAL**: That part of you that
   dreams up adventures, businesses and creative worlds, is
   sacred. It is the light that will actually guide you to an
   unexpected and beautiful future when you follow it. With
   the right self-knowledge and support, your own creativity
   and vision will be the best map towards a fulfilling future.
   Never dim your light for anyone. Ninety-nine of your
   fantasies may fall flat, but that one that works? It makes
   everything worth it.

Reframing the Lie

Instead of this:

~~I quit everything I start.~~

Try this:
I am multi-passionate.
I deserve to work at a job I enjoy.

"It's Okay to Change Direction"

Written by Rich

When I met Rox, I had been in the same job for *twenty years*. I'd worked my way up from a bank teller to a manager at one of the UK's largest banks. On our second date, this led to a very interesting conversation:

Rox: So how many other jobs have you had other than the bank?

Me: None. I've actually worked there from the time I was 16! How about you? How many jobs have you had?

Rox: Oh, wow . . . One job? Well, my life is going to sound insane after that . . .

Me: Go on. Tell me.

Rox: Fish 'n' chip shop, checkout girl . . . I've worked in loads of pubs over the years. Did a stint at a cancer charity and a bank. I trained to be an accountant for a couple of months, worked as a personal assistant, worked for a DJ, worked for a record label, ran a management company, was a singer/ songwriter for a bit, did some freelance graphic design, events marketing . . . I'm sure there are loads more I've forgotten.

Me: That is a comprehensive CV right there. If you don't mind me asking, how come you've had so many jobs?

Rox: I quit everything I start, in all honesty. It's not a trait I am proud of, but it's the truth.

I watched her shoulders slump down as this wonderful, vivacious, kind, hilarious person I was getting to know was overcome with embarrassment. She later confessed to me that she truly thought I wouldn't want to stay in touch with her because she felt like such a loser. Truth is, I didn't know why this awesome little emo with blue hair was interested in a boring bank manager! It's crazy how we always seem to devalue our own choices, isn't it?

Anyway, with the help of her therapist and some support from me, Rox made some pretty amazing life decisions and has been steadily working as a singer/songwriter for the last few years. It's the one job that she never lost the love for, her forever fixation. With the right support at home, and the professional support to work on a lot of trauma from her past, Rox found stability. But that part of her that was always looking for something new, seeking novelty, and impulsively changing direction is still with us. It just presents differently. And I had to learn this pretty quickly . . .

One day last year, there was a knock at the door. I opened it to see a delivery driver holding three large parcels.

"Babe, any idea what these are?" I asked Rox, who was dashing eagerly to the door.

"No idea," she said, taking them and ripping the packaging off.

"Ahh—my boots!" Rox squealed. She began piling an assortment of leather footwear and tools onto our kitchen table. She had ordered these things a while back and then promptly forgotten about them.

"What's going on here, babe?"

"I'm going to start customising footwear for goths!"

And that was that. For the next two weeks our kitchen became a workshop. Rox bustled around, punching holes and adding spikes and chains to her shoes. Painting flowers and love hearts on the side. She was totally consumed by her new business venture. Customising was all she could talk about. She devoured a steady diet of YouTube videos to learn the proper techniques, and each new creation made her immensely proud and happy.

Until one day, it didn't. The joy went out of her, and the business slowly began to wind down before even making its first sale. I noticed that she seemed to be embarrassed that things hadn't worked out as planned, that the excited promises and plans that had been the talk of our house had evaporated.

"Babe, what happened with the boots?"

"There's no dopamine there anymore."

"Say no more."

I gathered up all the tools and equipment and moved them to what we lovingly call the hobbies graveyard, moving a pot of resin and a soap-making kit to make room for them. Although Rox seemed embarrassed, as I said, there's no shame from me whatsoever when Rox stops something, because there is no expectation that things will last forever. Hobbies are there for fun, for as long as they last. That said, we've had to work hard to get here, however. Both of us have had to push for more understanding.

You see, Rox and I are polar opposites when it comes to choosing what projects we decide to start. For me it looks like this:

1. Do I have time?
2. How much do I want to do this?
3. What would I need to sacrifice to do it?

4. Does it make sense to do it?

5. Then, if all these questions are answered satisfactorily in my own head, I make a decision and commit to it.

For Rox, there is no such questioning. The minute the idea lands, it's being created. Equipment is being bought; domain names are being registered. I never, ever saw her as someone who was a quitter. (Other than the fact she quit drinking alcohol before we met. Let's not forget that quitting certain things can absolutely turn your life around!) I simply saw her as highly creative, perhaps a little impulsive, someone who didn't mind spending money or time on creative pursuits.

What I finally figured out was that Rox's challenge was not actually *quitting*. It was *starting*. I saw the pattern clear as day: a new hyperfixation would drop; she would be obsessed with it and totally consumed; she would spend time and money on it; and then she would over-commit, become overwhelmed, and then have to walk away—and once again, she'd feel like a failure. I knew that if I could get Rox to start fewer things, she would logically end up quitting less frequently.

So, how the hell do you get a passionate, wide-eyed ADHDer, someone who is flooded with dopamine about some new idea, to stop? Here is the three-part system I use to help Rox:

1. First, help them to differentiate between *dreaming* about the thing and *doing* the thing. Often, Rox gets as much joy from planning something as she gets from actually doing it—if not more. It's all of the creativity without the hard work. It's all the fun without the problems. That's the first port of call.

2. Next, get in the zone with them. Honestly, I think listening to and engaging in new hyperfixations should be an ADHD "love language." For Rox and me, that means that we'll lay

out that we're just going to plan and fantasise, but without actually doing anything (like buying equipment, or applying for a new job).

3. Finally, if your ADHDer is still feeling strongly that they need to act on their idea, use the following checklist. This has helped Rox and me to weed out so many amazing but ill-timed, expensive or not-quite-right business ideas. It's saved her a ton of money and time. And she has never had to start and fail anything.

Questions to Ask:

1. Does this idea align with your life purpose?
2. How much does this cost?
3. Do you have time in your life to truly dedicate to this?
4. Does this idea play to your strengths?
5. Is this idea ADHD-friendly?
6. Can this idea sustain your interest for a long period of time?
7. Are you willing to sacrifice current projects to make time for this one?
8. Would you be able to make decent money in the end?

By the time we have finished these questions, Rox has often convinced herself that an idea is actually best left in the planning stage. And when an idea passes this test, she sticks to it. This book is a perfect example of that.

How to Help an ADHDer Who Believes They Quit Everything They Start

The ADHD brain is set up for novelty, so we want to make sure novelty is encouraged and celebrated. *But* . . . we also want to be there to have honest conversations with them to help them evaluate potentially life-changing new ideas. ADHDers start so many things because they are so creative and driven! That is actually pretty amazing. But starting too many things inevitably leads to quitting, and that's where we can help.

Here's a few tips to help them quit quitting:

1. **REMEMBER, THERE'S NO SHAME IN QUITTING**: Your ADHDer's brain is set up for novelty. If their job isn't providing that, it can be an act of self-care to look for something new, if they are able to do so. There is no shame in quitting things that do not nurture or serve us. How many people work a job they hate for the majority of their life and end up regretting it? The discomfort ADHDers can feel is actually a great road map to making sure they live a life they are proud of.

2. **HELP YOUR ADHDer WITH SENSE-CHECKING**: Never try and stop your ADHDer's fantasy life and imagination. These are a huge source of excitement and joy. In addition, the vision they hold for the future can actually lead them (and sometimes you!) to some remarkable places. They are creative, driven and passionate, and all of these are incredibly valuable traits. Where we can help is just sense-checking ideas with them as they come up, using the questions I suggested on p. 68, to make sure they are viable. Honest conversations with your ADHDer can often lead to them making the decision themselves that now may not be the right time to pursue something.

3. **LOOK FOR ACCOMMODATIONS**: One reason Rox has been able to find stability for such a long stretch of time in her current job is that she has a lot of accommodations in place. She takes time off to recharge.

Her work colleagues know she has ADHD, so certain behaviours are supported. She has help with admin, for example. Of course, not all ADHDers have access to these supports. But more and more businesses and schools offer them these days. Accommodations can be a game-changer to stop an ADHDer feeling overwhelmed and they are always worth discussing and requesting.

4. **SHARE YOUR ADHDer's FANTASIES**: Jump into the fantasy of a new job or creative venture with your ADHDer. Let their mind wander wherever it needs to go. Sometimes just sharing this space is enough of a dopamine hit, and they won't actually want to pursue it any further. It's an amazing way to test your imagination and have fun together! Some people love playing board games or going rock-climbing. A lot of ADHDers *dream* for fun. Try making a game out of life and all its endless possibilities— much less frustrating than Monopoly.

Reframing the Lie

When they say this:
~~I quit everything I start.~~

Try telling them this:
It's okay to change direction.
There isn't one path to success.

ADHD Lie #4: I Am Stupid

Written by Rox

My whole adult life, I have been plagued by a sense of my own stupidity. I imagined that, perhaps, sometime around age 12 or 13, my peers had been taken aside and given a copy of a manual, and told not to ever share it with me. The contents of this mysterious book would have looked something like this:

THE NEUROTYPICAL MANUAL TO LIFE

Including chapters on:

- How to keep a tidy room (and not resort to a floordrobe)
- How to budget effectively (and not live on the edge of your overdraft)
- How to get through tasks in a timely fashion (rather than leaving them till the last possible moment)
- How to do laundry (and remember to actually take it out of the machine . . .)
- How to behave in a social situation (rather than staring awkwardly between somebody's eyes)
- How to stay in touch with friends (and actually reply to text messages)
- How to put together IKEA furniture (without having a mental breakdown)

I would picture their parents reading it to them every night before bed, answering any questions in full, and using visual work-throughs to ensure they understood how to tackle all these basic but absolutely necessary key life skills.

"Is everything clear now, Johnny?" the loving parent would ask the attentive teen. "It's really important you can understand and apply this if you are going to take care of yourself in the future."

In all seriousness, though, I wish there *was* a secret manual. At least that would have explained why I didn't understand how to do *anything* and why I struggled. Alas, there is no secret manual (although I'm still suspicious). So, the only logical conclusion I could draw in the face of everybody else's flourishing and my failing was that I was just incredibly stupid.

Oddly, though, as a young child, I didn't believe I was stupid at all. When I was 11, for instance, I was already working on logic puzzles with my parents. I did them with such ease that they began to suspect me of being gifted—an interesting and positive-sounding label. Looking back now, though, I can't help but wonder if what they were actually witnessing was ADHD: the problem solving, the hyperfocus, the creativity. They were noticing all the things society saw as a benefit, but not seeing any of the struggles that came with them. Logic puzzles lit up my young brain. My hyperfocus would switch on and I would see nothing else until I had found the answer. Naturally, I was praised for being "extremely bright" for my age, and began to believe that this was my value in life: being smart. That, I decided, was how I would get people to love and respect me.

Similarly, in school I was distracted and often labelled as troublesome, but come exam time I could walk out with straight As after a long night of obsessive hyperfocusing on the textbooks that I was opening for the first time. The intense pressure of the upcoming 9 a.m. exam would kick me into a mode of super-focus! I was able to read large chunks of text and retain the information. Essentially accessing a part of my memory that I normally couldn't. Come the next day I would be able to write out answers, almost word for word. I never really understood what I was working on; I merely saw it as a game of beating the system. Of remembering as much as I could. Now that I understand ADHD, and how urgency can motivate us, I fully understand what I was doing: I was waiting until the last possible moment to act because I needed the stress and extreme pressure to be able to work effectively. Of course, at the time I had no idea any of this was happening.

My core belief as a kid was *"I am very bright and destined for great things."* Fast forward to being 25, living in a pigsty of a flat, in mountains of debt, behind on bills, and with a number of failed job attempts under my belt. The fall from grace was pretty spectacular.

I have got so many stories of stupid things I have done in my life. In the name of shame-busting, I'm going to share one of the ones I am most mortified about, which happened in my twenties on a trip home. Often the full extent of ADHD symptoms isn't recognised until a child moves out.

"There is a lot of mail for you . . ."

My dad handed me a stack of about 100 letters. White and brown envelopes, many of them featuring that dreaded red label, "Urgent." Although I had technically moved out of home at 18, and was now 26 and living somewhere in West London, I had never updated any of my new addresses. So, any important correspondence would never reach me; rather, it was sent directly to my dad. He'd collect these letters for me and hand them over the next time I dropped by . . . usually unplanned.

The reason why I never updated my address even now fills me with a profound sense of sadness. You see, I never stayed in one place for very long. Nowhere really felt like home. No matter where I was, I felt like I was only passing through. Often, I didn't even bother to unpack my suitcase. Why go through all the trouble of changing addresses at banks and doctors if I'd be moving in a few months anyway? Not to mention the fact that admin tasks like this can feel pretty impossible for an ADHD brain! The constant moving was a reflection of my ever-changing jobs, and my even more ever-changing relationships. I was constantly on the run, never quite willing to settle down anywhere.

So back to the stack of envelopes marked "Urgent." Sitting on my old bedroom floor, now converted into my stepmother's dressing room, I began to open my mail. There was no way I'd get through all of it, so I decided to play "red letter roulette," choosing a few envelopes at random. Better than nothing.

- A phone bill from three years ago that had been handed over to debt collectors. Fantastic.
- A reminder for my annual smear test that I had never had.
- A letter informing me I had lost my driving licence.

Hold on—that last one couldn't be right. I read it again:

Due to multiple offences totalling over the allowed points we regret to inform you your licence has been revoked. You will need to take both your theory and practical tests before you are able to drive again.[8]

Oh fuck. I almost threw up onto the synthetic red rug. I needed my car to get to work. To travel. I'd be lost without it. My eyes glazing over with frustration and fear, I began scanning the letter again for any sign that this might be reversible. The thought that I could have been driving around without a licence, or valid insurance, endangering other people, filled me with horror.

I am so fucking stupid.

In the end, I had to sell my car and take the train back up to London. I was now relegated to tubes and buses once more. As I write this, more than ten years later, I still don't have a driving licence. Retaking my theory test, driving lessons, the test itself . . . it all involves so much admin, so much organization that I simply don't have in me. That can make someone feel pretty stupid as an adult—being unable to accomplish what most barely-out-of-school 18-year-olds do.

But the reason why I never updated my address, or struggled to book in driving lessons was not intellectual—it was because of ADHD.

There are two key parts of ADHD that can make us feel stupid:

- **Working memory issues**: this manifests as a constant forgetfulness, even of things you have just been told or information you have just read.
- **Executive function challenges**: difficulties with knowing how to get started, how to organize thoughts in your own mind and execute plans.

The scientific definitions always lack a little spice for me, however, so let's make it more personal. Here are the things I do regularly, that historically I would have thought of as stupid, but are actually related to ADHD:

- Forgetting countless appointments and calls with work.
- Leaving my bag on the train.
- Leaving my shopping at the shop.
- Leaving my phone at the shop.
- Losing my phone while it's in my hand.
- Walking into a room and forgetting why I'm there.
- Leaving the oven on.
- Getting lost, especially if I'm going somewhere important.
- Missing my stop on the train.
- Going the wrong way on the train.
- Losing my headphones numerous times.
- Losing my wallet numerous times.

That's what ADHD looks like in real life. What working memory and executive function challenges add up to. At times, it can feel like an absolute shit show. Constantly losing things, forgetting things, going in the wrong direction, and arriving at the wrong places. After a while, it begins to wear on you—the shame of it all; the exhaustion. The cringey-ness of having to tell someone you are running late again, or the expense of having to buy a tenth pair of headphones. That's why we need to talk about it.

Now I know this, instead of my fearleader, there is a new voice in my head:

"Can you shut up? This isn't stupidity, and you aren't helping."

This is what I like to call my inner defender, taking up their ADHD shield against my inner critic.

The "I'm stupid" narrative was nothing more than the result of having a neurodevelopmental condition and trying to function like I didn't.

Looking back on pre-diagnosis-me I am filled with compassion. If I could go back in time and body-double myself whilst I did crucial life admin I would!

Believing this lie steals something incredibly important from us: the self-esteem and confidence that comes from possessing intelligence. But there are many different types of intelligence! I bet you possess loads of skills that other people you know do not. I wonder . . . would you call them stupid if they struggled with something you found easy? It's time we offered ourselves the same freedom that we offer neurotypicals; with the belief that different human beings have very different skills. ADHDers may struggle with what society may call "basic" skills, but we will excel in other areas of intellect. Let's not define ourselves by our challenges, but rather by our unique skills.

Unlearning the "I Am Stupid" Lie

Living in a neurotypical world as someone with ADHD is going to make you feel stupid. You will struggle with things many other people do without thinking, and your only explanation will be that it is your fault. It creates a toxic place within your own mind, as you repeat what the world has been reflecting back to you from a young age: There is something wrong with you. You are stupid.

The truth is, calling yourself stupid for struggling with a neurodevelopmental condition is as nonsensical as calling someone with a broken leg lazy for not walking properly. You cannot help it. You are not doing it on purpose. And no amount of bullying—from yourself, or others—is going to change that. So, rather than focusing on your limitations, you must learn to advocate and accommodate for your disability, so you can fully apply yourself to areas of your life where you do possess amazing gifts and talents.

Here's a list to help you with that:

1. **NEVER SAY "STUPID"**: Another word to add to the ban list. Don't say it to yourself. And don't allow others to say it to you. It is imperative that you build a shield to protect yourself from a world that is set up to make you feel inferior. If you lose your way, forget something, lose something, or make an impulsive mistake, label those things that way. Do not assign moral values to them. A symptom of ADHD is hard enough to deal with without the constant negative commentary.

2. **ORGANIZED DOESN'T MEAN CLEVER**: Forgo the belief that being good at admin automatically makes somebody of higher intelligence. Being good at admin is just that. Nothing more. There is no moral or intellectual value to assign to it. Just like some people are great at spreadsheets, you too have your strengths. That is the diversity of humanity, and it is a beautiful thing. Look for all of the other skills that you possess that make you unique.

3. **NURTURE YOUR SELF-ESTEEM**: A lifetime of perceived failure at easy tasks will erode your sense of self-esteem. Rebuilding it will take time and effort. Self-esteem is built through doing something you can feel proud of. It's unlikely that what broke us will be the thing to fix us. So, we need to look for other places to build self-esteem, for instance: great parenting and relationships, creativity, friendship, art classes, the gym, content creation. Finding things that you love to work on, committing to them, and

watching yourself thrive, will start to shift the narrative and allow you to see that there are places where your unique brain can actually give you an advantage.

4. **DEVELOP AN ADHD SHIELD**: You must develop an inner protector. A voice inside your own head that will stand up and say, "Hey, this is just a consequence of ADHD. This is not stupidity." You have likely lived with a bully in your mind for so many years; it will take time and practice to cultivate the protective voice! So be patient with yourself. The next time you lose something, can't understand something, or forget something, practise speaking kindly and compassionately to yourself in your own mind. We must learn to be kind to ourselves internally, so we can then begin protecting ourselves in the outside world! There are already plenty of people who want to label us as "stupid." Don't become one of them.

Reframing the Lie

Instead of this:
~~I am stupid.~~

Try this:
I struggle with certain things due to my condition.
I also have lots of skills that others don't have.

"You're Not Stupid"

Written by Rich

The first time I witnessed Rox's skills in the cleaning department was when we were moving out of the flat that we had shared for just three months. She had moved into my place, so I had just kept my routine going as normal. Meaning I never saw what she was hiding under her bonnet in terms of her cleaning techniques . . .

We'd agreed to do a deep clean of the flat, rather than hire a company to do it. Looking back now, and knowing how deeply she loathes and struggles with cleaning, I see that she must have been petrified! I guess that is the power of new love. It makes you do loads of crazy things. Including cleaning!

I was getting on with my tasks around the flat, and Rox had said she'd clean the kitchen. She'd been at it for about half an hour when I walked in to check her progress. The floor, the surfaces and her were completely soaked. She was holding onto a dripping sponge, manically cleaning anything she could see. Sweat was dripping off her forehead. It looked like there had been a leak in there.

"Wow, babe," I said. "That is a lot of water! I reckon it might help if you wrung out the sponge."

"God, why didn't I think of that?" she said, defeated. "Sorry. I'm so stupid."

That sentence would take on a life of its own over the coming year. Every time Rox struggled or made a mistake, she would turn in on herself—calling herself stupid, or inept, or incompetent. Even before her ADHD diagnosis, I would never, ever have used those terms to describe her. She was definitely a bit haphazard, a bit forgetful, a bit accident-prone. But certainly not stupid.

If anything, Rox seemed super-smart to me. She was always whizzing around the house, decorating hallways, writing songs, painting jackets, re-arranging furniture. She was constantly alight with amazing creative energy. Okay, not constantly. Sometimes she was buried deep in an interest: hunkered down in a cosy fort of blankets, wearing PJs, scrolling the internet. But you get the idea . . . This person wasn't stupid. She was actually very bright, if a bit prone to organizational errors.

I remember vividly the panicked phone call I got at 8:00 one evening. I was meant to be picking Rox up from Sevenoaks train station. The minute I answered the phone, I heard the familiar fear in her voice.

"I'm going to Tunbridge Wells. I've missed my stop. I don't know what to do."

A few calming words, a quick Google search, and we were sorted. I was driving to Tunbridge Wells to meet her. No harm done. Of course, Rox had been stewing about her own stupidity for the rest of the journey, and she arrived at the station extremely embarrassed, upset and profusely apologetic.

"God, I am so sorry you've had to come all this way. I'm so stupid. I'm so sorry."

I sometimes wonder if the way Rox spoke about herself was a defense mechanism: almost like attacking herself before anybody else had the chance to. If she apologised enough times and called herself horrible names, then I wouldn't be angry with her. The thing is, I was never angry at her. It was very obvious she wasn't doing any of this stuff on purpose. Who would want to be waiting at a cold Kentish train station when they could be wrapped up watching the latest season of *Love Is Blind?*

Mistakes like this were pretty common pre-diagnosis. And they showed up in many different areas—forgotten anniversaries, dropped plates, lost headphones, lost wallets, missed trains. We couldn't get through a day without her doing something she deemed utterly unacceptable. It's the ADHD diagnosis that was the turning point for both of us. Finally, we had a language with which we could talk about what was happening, rather than her simply blaming herself. It took time and practice, though. Rox had to learn to move away from the self-punishment she had used forever, and I had to learn to call out this "small talk" behaviour and encourage self-compassion instead. After a while, there was a really beautiful, yet subtle shift in the way that she spoke to me. And I think a lot of you will recognise it.

It was the shift from "I'm sorry" to "thank you."

ADHDers often apologise for their symptoms and behaviours, and for the consequences of their struggles. After a lifetime of living in a world that reflects back to them that they are failing and stupid, a burden to the rest of us, "sorry" becomes an armour against that kind of judgment. They swoop in to take the blame for everything before someone else has the chance to reject them and their behaviour. In a supported environment, one that is free of judgment and also high on accommodations, an ADHDer will stop blaming themselves for their condition. Instead, they will say thank you when they receive support and guidance.

Nowadays, when Rox drops or loses something, it's much more common for her to thank me for my reaction, help or support. That little language shift means she is never apologising for things she can't help, and is recognising how much she appreciates the non-judgmental environment.

Rox has often said that she wishes she could be more like me. More organized. Better with admin, planning, finances and all that boring stuff. Truth is, I look at her and wish the same thing! I envy her ability to get totally lost in a new hobby, to create something, or to research and learn about new topics, not to mention that she is the emotional glue that holds our family together. When one of the kids is feeling something, she's the first to notice. She will never shy away from a tough conversation and always encourages us to be open about what we're going through. She helps us navigate conflict, and is so open with her own emotions that it's had a knock-on effect for all of us. Before Rox was in my life, although I saw myself as a good dad, I definitely wasn't emotionally available in the way I am now. Neurodivergent people are often highly sensitive, which makes them very skilled at empathy and communication—and emotional intelligence.

Over the last few years, with therapy, an ADHD diagnosis, and a pretty awesome partner (ha!), I have watched her flourish. She's become absolutely amazing at work, and has finally found success in a career she has wanted to pursue for many years. Her ADHD is part of our day-to-day life, and our home is full of acceptance. And the occasional late-night pick-up from a random train station.

But ADHD also allows her to be deeply connected to her life's purpose, to envision a future and create that world, to create art and messages that can truly change people's lives.

So often our world seems to focus on what ADHD people lack, and how they need to force themselves to become neurotypical by any means possible. What I've learned is that nothing will "fix" ADHD. And in fact, trying to fix it often makes things worse. A temporary improvement in symptoms leads to overworking, which leads to burnout, which leads to feeling stupid once again. Struggling with organization, time-keeping and directions can not only lead the ADHDer to question their intelligence, but also everyone around them. We can all be so consumed with what they are not getting right, we miss other types of intelligence they possess in bucketloads!

Intelligence isn't about how organized you are. There are many different types of intelligence, including emotional skills and creativity. It's time we started valuing the incredible intelligence of many neurodivergent people, while also supporting their struggles with some "basic" functions.

How to Help an ADHDer Who Believes They're Stupid

After a lifetime of struggling with things others find easy, your ADHDer likely has a deep-rooted sense that they are stupid. They may struggle to understand why they can't process time, emails or administration like other people seem to, and they probably see this as a personal failing.

The key to changing this core belief is to emphasise that "being organized" (although very helpful) is not a moral prerequisite to living a happy full life and pursuing your own passions and dreams. To unlock the gifts within someone with ADHD so that they can self-actualise and build real self-esteem in this world, we have to help them stop their small-talking and toxic self-bullying, and help them change that core belief that they are stupid when they struggle with a task because of their condition.

Here are some tips to help you help them:

1. **REMIND THEM THEY HAVE ADHD**: When your ADHDer is struggling with something, remind them that they have ADHD! Working memory problems might actually get in the way of what they're trying to do, and even after a diagnosis they may forget to even consider this. Gently and kindly remind the person that there are reasons for certain behaviours that absolutely don't make them stupid. It just makes them somebody with ADHD.

2. **FOCUS ON THE GENIUS**: ADHDers will have multiple interests and areas of amazing skill. For instance, they might be calm in crisis, learn new skills quickly, or be able to come up with incredible creative ideas. They have lived for a long time in a world that points to their flaws, so be the person who points out their value and their skills. With the right support and understanding, people with ADHD can add amazing value and diversity to our world.

3. **NO BULLYING**: If you heard someone screaming at a loved one that they were stupid, you would likely intervene with some "firm" words. Seeing someone you love get bullied is a horrible experience. This is also true if they are the ones doing the bullying. Call it out any time they call themselves stupid. Remind them it isn't okay to speak to themselves like that, and push them to find a compassionate way to view themselves instead.

4. **PRAISE THEM**: Your ADHDer has likely been shamed for making mistakes their whole life, while their amazing

gifts have gone undervalued and unnoticed. Genuine praise can go a long way towards counteracting this. When you see them doing something they find easy, praise the unique life skills and sensibilities they've brought to the task. It's also important to praise their effort towards things they find hard. If Rox cleans the bedroom, is ready on time, or manages to get through a difficult task, I will make a point of noticing it, and we'll celebrate together. People with ADHD have often been starved of celebration for their successes, big and small.

Reframing the Lie

When they say this:

~~I am stupid.~~

Try telling them this:
You have loads of different skills.
You don't deserve to feel awful about things you can't help.

ADHD Lie #5: ADHD Isn't Real, I'm Just a Bad Person

Written by Rox

I remember the first time I ever heard the four-letter abbreviation that would go on to become the explanation of my *entire* life, and in fact turn into my job.

"ADHD is just what middle-class parents call their kids instead of saying they are lazy."

One of my relatives was sharing their thoughts with us around the family dining table. I was 13 at the time.

I don't blame this relative for their views. They grew up in the 1950s before ADHD was even a diagnosis! We simply didn't have as much knowledge and awareness as we do now. ADHD was associated mainly with hyperactive boys, and even then, it was an unusual diagnosis. I wasn't missed on purpose; I simply didn't fit the understanding that most people had about it. In my family's eyes I was just a bit lazy, forgetful, rebellious and impulsive. There was no other way to interpret my behaviour.

I feel very sorry for relatives, parents and carers of late-diagnosed children, who are perhaps having to reckon with the fact they treated their child with judgment and frustration. Finding out neurodivergence was behind a child's behaviour may induce a lot of guilt. However, it's not the past that defines us, but the future. Carers who choose to learn, to support their children now, and to do better because they know better, are heroes in my eyes.

The second time I would hear the term ADHD was in my therapist's office—at age 36. We had spent many months working through my unprocessed grief over my mum's death, and the CPTSD (complex PTSD) symptoms that I had been living with: vivid emotional flashbacks, hypervigilance and a total lack of personal identity. I was coming back to myself for the first time. Learning to cry, to find my own voice, to connect with the long-repressed rage inside me. It was incredibly painful, terribly lonely, and it also saved my life. Things gradually began to get better. I practised breathing exercises regularly to take my body out of its fight-or-flight response and began to address the patterns of behaviour that had dominated my life.

It was only after the smog had cleared from some of my more serious mental health issues that my ADHD symptoms became more evident. They'd been buried under years and years of rubble. I wouldn't have noticed them in my twenties, for example, because everything was a mess. I was an alcoholic, a relationship addict, and I was changing jobs and partners like the wind. In the same way you wouldn't notice a broken light in a house on fire, I had to put out the fire before I could start to see something else was at play.

Up until this point I had always blamed my behaviour on just being a bad person. Losing things because I was a drunk, having emotional meltdowns because I was a brat, being disorganized because I was stupid. After I'd made some massive progress in therapy, I told my therapist about some strange things I had begun to notice.

"Listen, Doc. I have been feeling a lot better recently. I don't feel constantly on edge. I am starting to feel safe at home for the first time. I am so happy with my progress . . . But I have noticed something weird: I'm missing a lot of trains, and losing a lot of things."

The doctor's next words surprised me.

"That potentially sounds like some attention deficit difficulties."

My mind raced back to the family dining table.

"ADHD is for middle-class kids who cannot accept they are lazy."

Unsurprisingly, something in me rejected the very notion that there might be something legitimately different about me. The story that I was the root cause of all of my problems had been around for a long time.

Luckily for me, I had an intense special interest in psychology. I had been obsessed with it for a number of years, and so the mere mention of ADHD lit up my brain! *DING DING DING!* Time for a new hyperfocus! Over the next few weeks, I fell into a whole world of ADHD content, books and podcasts. Every single one re-affirmed back to me that, in fact, all of those unique and often quite shameful behaviours I had suffered with my whole life were actually a universal experience of people with ADHD. The consequence of a condition. I wasn't alone. There were many of us out there!

I was incredibly privileged to be able to pursue a diagnosis via private healthcare, which was offered to Rich by his employer at the time. A few hour-long Zoom calls, and there it was. The starting point to beginning to understand myself for the first time. I am beyond grateful for that access, and I know so many people reading this will be on months- or years-long waiting lists as they attempt to get the same life-changing and affirming diagnosis that I was given. If that is you, I want you to know something: self-diagnosis is a prerequisite to official diagnosis. It was my own research and obsessions about these symptoms and struggles that allowed me to finally get an official diagnosis. If you have done your research and strongly believe you have ADHD, there is absolutely no harm in following people and reading books that may offer suggestions that help you and make you feel understood.

Of course, there are many comorbidities—that means conditions that can exist alongside ADHD. For me that was CPTSD. I have friends who are AuDHD (autism and ADHD) and who also have OCD (obsessive-compulsive disorder) and other conditions. Everyone deserves the right to discuss these issues and any others with a professional, but unfortunately, we live in a world where access isn't always possible. No one should feel like they cannot access community resources. You are very welcome here no matter your diagnosis status.

Interestingly, after my diagnosis, I was met with a rather maddening consequence: a deep, internal sense that the doctor was wrong. That I didn't have ADHD but had somehow convinced them that I did. Or that my test had come out wrong. They *had* to be wrong, I told myself, because I knew without doubt that I was actually just a bad person. "You cannot tell me I have a condition that explains the majority of my struggles," I argued in my head. "That is such an easy way out. I *need* to struggle. I *need* to fail. I *need* to beat myself up. That's the way it's always been."

Part of the reason I believe we started our social media accounts (aside from an impulsive late-night ADHD-infused decision) was that I was desperately trying to hold on to this diagnosis. To make it real. I want you to know, that even after two years of creating daily content, doing constant research, getting feedback from a community, and writing our second book, there is still a voice inside me that questions the validity of my diagnosis. That wants to say, "No. That is not for you."

Ninety-nine percent of the comments we receive online are wonderful—people sharing their own stories of ADHD woes, realising for the first time that they might have ADHD, and generally experiencing the "I thought it was just me" shock!

But then there's the remaining 1 percent, the negative comments, which are very creative and cover a range of topics. Here are some of our regulars:

- "Shave your armpits. You are disgusting."
- "She looks like a man without makeup. Poor bloke."
- "How the hell does he live with that?"
- "She needs to grow up. How pathetic."
- . . . and the ever-popular "ADHD isn't real."

Most of the time, I'm able to laugh these off. Okay, maaaaybe—just maybe—my immediate reaction is rage and a desire to find the person's address, but that passes after a few seconds. I remind myself that people leaving hateful comments probably aren't living the happiest lives themselves, and I simply block and delete. But the last one always gets me: "ADHD isn't real." That one troubles me. It hangs out like a bad smell long after I have blocked and deleted.

It's interesting to note that often the criticisms that hurt us the most are the things that, on some subconscious level, we believe ourselves. ADHD had become a saving grace for me. A reason to understand myself not as some awful failing mess, but as someone who just needed a bit of support in certain areas. It has saved my relationship by giving us language and context to discuss how it showed up and affected us. It has given me a career, a community, and a way to truly add value to this little world. But deep down, I was still haunted by the idea that it wasn't real.

ADHD advocacy and awareness is a rather interesting place to be when you have an unkind inner voice telling you that it isn't even real. Within our community there are wildly different takes on where ADHD comes from, how it develops, and how to deal with it. It becomes extremely confusing when there's not just one answer for something, one truth to hold on to. Even the scientific community does not always agree on ADHD. Some doctors don't think it is real at all (thankfully now in the minority!), saying it is actually just a cluster of other symptoms. Some doctors say it is purely genetic. Some say it can be made worse by traumatic events. So, if even doctors cannot agree, what hope is there for us?

The truth is, I don't need to know if ADHD is genetic. If it may have been made worse by trauma. If it's purely neurodevelopmental. I don't even need it to be called ADHD. In all honesty, ADHD is a terrible name for it. I don't have a deficit of attention; as I said in *Dirty Laundry*, I have the total opposite: a wild, uncontrollable attention. My biggest struggle isn't trying to focus, or that I lose things, or struggle with time. It's actually the chronically low self-esteem about my abilities I have been living with my whole life, and all of the negative core beliefs that I hold.

What nobody can ever take away is that the symptoms are real. And that the consequences of living undiagnosed can be devastating. That is the most important part. Millions of people, deeply suffering, with the same problems. I can see the evidence of it. I can see the life-changing shifts from self-hatred to acceptance when people finally get the tools they need. I have seen what has happened in my own life: my first healthy relationship, some actual success at work, and, more importantly, an end to the constant inner bullying I have subjected myself to.

Those denying the existence of ADHD, or saying it is trendy and over-diagnosed, will certainly get plenty of attention for their views online. Social media is set up to reward controversy. The hotter the take, the more likely it will be to hit a million views. The fact that ADHD has become such a controversial topic means that it absolutely will be used to sell newspapers, get documentary views, and pick up cheap clicks. Just because somebody shares a harmful opinion, does not mean we have to engage in it.

Your struggles. Your story. Your voice. Your experience. These things cannot be invalidated by anyone. Not by user98886655544 shouting into the TikTok void that "ADHD is just an excuse for being lazy." Not by TV channels deciding to run a scaremongering documentary on whether "ADHD is being over-diagnosed."

We ADHDers are here. We have wet laundry in the dryer. We have a thousand unread texts. And we are trying to stop hating ourselves. Nothing anyone says stops us from existing, or stops our symptoms from being very real.

I think back to my relative's view of ADHD, which filtered down into my own, and often wonder whether that is a big part of the backlash we are seeing: people who were never given true care and support, lashing out at those who are. It's also probably why ADHD-deniers can be so triggering to us. Perhaps on a deeper level they remind us of an unsympathetic relative.

A Word about ADHD and People of Color

In all the uproar about the overdiagnosis of ADHD, the world misses something very important: that people of color, or POC, are still massively underdiagnosed in comparison to white people.[9] They are more likely to be labelled as "disruptive" and never offered the diagnosis and treatment that could help them, due to racial disparity. Think about the people with ADHD that you follow online. Think about the people with ADHD who have been platformed by the mainstream media. They are pretty much all white.[10]

I am part of the "late-diagnosed women" community. There are swathes of us now finally getting the understanding and support we have missed out on our whole life. We can see clearly why we were missed, why it was little white boys who were the accepted face of ADHD, and the negative consequences that had on us. The same thing is happening again to POC. They are being left out of the conversation and representation, making it harder for them to access life-changing support.

As a community we have work to do. We must reach out to those who have historically been left out of the conversation, be they women, POC, or other marginalised groups. Our time is better spent building community, sharing our stories, and uplifting others than arguing with some old dude on the internet.

Unlearning the "ADHD Isn't Real, I'm Just a Bad Person" Lie

It is common for people with ADHD to doubt the validity of their own diagnosis. Particularly if they were diagnosed later in life. You have a lifetime of evidence telling you that you are, in fact, just a bad person. Accepting an ADHD diagnosis will feel like an easy way out, a lazy way out, a way to avoid accountability. This can make getting the support you need very difficult.

I imagine many of you reading this book have thousands of unread emails, at least one text you dread opening, and of course doom piles scattered over the house! In fact, you are probably reading this book instead of doing something else you are meant to be doing! We have a common, lived, real experience of ADHD. We know that diagnosis is often the turning point for somebody finding happiness for the first time in their life, as the veil of shame lifts and they are able to be kind to themselves. It's natural to doubt an ADHD diagnosis. That doesn't mean you don't have ADHD, or that ADHD isn't real. It means you have been living your whole life blaming yourself, and that it feels alien to have a medical reason for your struggles.

Here are some ways to help you accept your ADHD:

1. **REBUILD YOUR IDENTITY**: When you discover you have ADHD, you can experience equal parts grief and joy. Grief at the years lost to struggle and self-hatred. And joy at finally having language to explain your struggles and what sort of help you need. Your identity has been built on the broken assumption that you are somehow deeply flawed. It is time to rebuild from the ground up, to create a new identity based on understanding, support and hope, not one based on personal failure. You're actually really bloody awesome! You just haven't allowed yourself to see it yet . . .

2. **BEWARE OF "DEBATES"**: So many of us have hyperfocused on ADHD. When something is so life-changing, it is common that we want to know everything about it. When you delve deep into ADHD within academic research, in mainstream media, or online, you will find a vast array of differing opinions. For every kind voice offering hope, there will be another one calling it a trend. Try not to obsess about these debates. It is enough to know

that ADHD is defined in the US handbook DSM-5 (*The Diagnostic and Statistical Manual of Mental Disorders*, Fifth Edition), and to know that you have it. The arguments and discussions can only serve as a distraction from working through the core beliefs that have developed and are holding you back.

3. **GO WHERE YOU ARE VALUED**: When you are unwinding a lifetime of "bad-person-itis," you need to surround yourself with people who see your value, your kindness, and your intentions. If you spend time with people who see you as a problem, an attention-seeker, an issue, there is no way you will be able to grow in self-acceptance. You will either take on their negative views of you, or you will exist in a constant state of defense against their attacks. Start to notice who wants to listen and learn, who cares about your story and your experience. And notice, too, who wants to belittle, condemn and ignore you. It might be time to limit certain people's access to you.

4. **DISTINGUISH BAD BEHAVIOUR FROM "BEING BAD"**: There is a big difference between bad behaviour and being a bad person. Bad behaviour offers a chance at redemption, at learning and growing. Being a bad person does not. It is a heavy burden to bear. I have done many bad things in my life, some related to ADHD and some not. I have started fights, broken hearts, and, more shamefully, driven drunk. I would never want to claim these behaviours aren't deserving of criticism. They are absolutely bad and should be addressed. But we must separate the behaviour from the person. Often, underneath difficult behaviours is somebody struggling with their mental health. We must lean into compassion and understanding, both for ourselves and for others.

Reframing the Lie

Instead of this:
~~ADHD isn't real, I'm just a bad person.~~

Try this:
I have ADHD, and often need more help than others.
I am deeply valuable despite the struggles that I have.

"You're Not a Bad Person"

Written by Rich

The day Rox actually got her ADHD diagnosis, we were going out for dinner. Rather comically, she was running late, darting around looking for her phone—which was in her hand—changing outfits at the last minute, and searching for her wallet. Flustered, she finally got into the passenger seat, twenty minutes later than planned. Historically, these moments could quickly escalate into panic attacks and a lot of self-shaming, but this time, something different was happening. It sounded like she was giggling . . .

. . . And then the giggling turned into howls of laughter. I had never seen her find something so funny. As her deep belly laughs rumbled through the car, I shut the windows so the neighbours wouldn't think something was wrong.

"Babe, what's so funny?"

Through peals of laughter, she squealed, "This is a condition!" She threw her head back and laughed even harder. I could almost feel the joy rolling off her. The sense that all of those historical mornings filled with struggles had a cause. The fact perhaps that losing her phone and wallet a million times was actually part of a set of diagnostic criteria. It all felt so silly . . . and so brilliant. Her joy and relief were infectious, and I started laughing too.

But then something changed. The hysterical laughter took on more of a painful undertone. Next thing I knew, she was sobbing.

"Bubby," I said, shocked, "what's going on?"

Through a snotty nose and tear-induced hiccups, she told me she had no idea.

Later, at dinner, when the emotions had passed, we were able to discuss what had happened. It was a phenomenon known as the grief and joy of diagnosis. We call it *groy* in our house. On the one hand, she had finally got an answer to the questions she (and others) had always asked: *What's wrong with me?*

She finally had a reason for why she struggled so much in certain areas but excelled in others. The constant lateness, the failures, the forgetting and losing things that have coloured her entire life was now explained in just four letters. ADHD.

For many people receiving this diagnosis, that moment can be joyful, and sometimes hilarious. But there is often also a kind of mourning for all of the years lost to self-hatred. Rox was grieving for all of the times she had been judged, and told she was not trying. There is tremendous sadness in the realisation that you have lived your whole life misunderstood and unsupported, and that perhaps the darkest days never actually needed to happen.

The *groy—simultaneous grief and joy*—of diagnosis is a rite of passage for an ADHDer. As their partner or parent, it's important for you to allow both sides of the emotional coin into the equation. They have been given the missing puzzle piece they have been searching for their whole lives, and it's absolutely life-changing! Their identity will be shifting on a very deep level, from someone who is broken to someone who deserves understanding. It will affect all areas of their life: how they show up in relationships, how they function at work, their self-talk, and their self-image.

In true ADHD fashion, Rox quickly became even more obsessed with the subject. Podcasts were on a constant loop, boxes of books were being delivered, and pretty much every conversation revolved around the new things she had discovered about herself. It's like who she was had always been locked behind a door, and someone had just given her the key.

In an ideal world, when somebody gets an ADHD diagnosis, that should be it. No more shaming. No more self-hatred. Friends and relatives will say, "Let's call this what it is and start getting the help you need." But humans are complicated creatures. And Rox was no exception.

She lived with a deep sense of personal badness that, despite all of her healing work, had never really loosened its grip on her. She was plagued constantly by the nagging thought that she was awful. Despicable. A fake. A fraud. And as our ADHD accounts began to grow on social media, so did her doubts. We would receive the odd comment that could send her on a downward spiral:

user8765003212: ADHD isn't real. This is just a spoilt brat that never grew up.

I watched Rox question herself:

> What if it isn't real?
> What if I don't have it?
> What if I faked it?
> What if I am just broken and this is an excuse?

Even with all those doubts circling round in her head, I found it amazing to watch Rox speaking to people we would meet on the streets. She would engage them in conversations about their value, and identify with their struggles. She was a totally committed advocate for ADHD, reminding other people of how freeing and wonderful it can be to get diagnosed, and sharing everything she has learned to find self-acceptance. Yet . . . deep down inside, she still struggled to allow herself full access to this compassion, to accept ADHD as part of her own identity.

I think perhaps this is a deeper problem for those who are diagnosed as adults. This is actually the fastest-growing demographic of ADHD at this moment: people who have lived their whole lives cobbling together strategies to get through, to try and stay on top of things. People who have inevitably been met with crushing failures and struggles in all areas of their lives. For these people, especially if they were unsupported, the deeply entrenched narrative is that they are fundamentally flawed. That they need to fix themselves. To stop being a burden on others. And to accept that they are just not as good as other humans.

The consequences of these beliefs are pretty devastating. Rox has a complicated history of addiction, self-harm, debt and broken relationships. I'm not saying that none of these things would have happened if her ADHD had been diagnosed and supported earlier, but I do imagine the really bad days might have been fewer. This is why it is so important that we learn about ADHD, and speak loudly about it to raise awareness. This will help parents and other care providers, to recognise the symptoms in their children, and get the support they deserve before the toxic self-belief that they are bad has had time to entrench itself in their souls.

I have had my own experiences of feeling like a bad person. I struggled with addiction through my twenties and early thirties. This involved gambling in secret, often spinning slots behind the wheel or in the toilets at work, losing vast amounts of money, and hiding it from my then wife. I remember once changing my baby daughter's nappy in the middle of the night and hiding out in her room afterwards to gamble. This was shameful behaviour, and truly, without recovery meetings and therapy I would have gone on living that way, believing I was bad to the core. Whatever you believe you are becomes your reality. So, when I hated myself, I acted in ways that supported that belief. I was a binge drinker, I had a temper, and I never asked for help. I was sexually abused when I was 8 years old and had never told anyone or had any therapy or help for it. In time I came to realise that much of my personal badness was born from my attempts to numb the pain of what had happened. It was only by speaking about it that I was able to get better.

Rox and I had that in common: childhood experiences that became internalised. Neither of us came from families that were able to speak about emotions, or validate experiences. Rather, our families believed it was better to ignore the tough stuff and chat about the neighbours' yellow grass instead. For both of us, our relationship proved a safe space to be able to open up completely and share the core wounds that had led to some of our difficult experiences.

A sense of being bad can rob you of your basic human dignity. It can stop you asking for help, kill any expectations of ever truly being loved, or realising your true potential. It's like a weed, slowly choking the life out of the flowers that are trying to bloom.

For those of us who love someone with ADHD, the diagnosis is just the first step, similar to when I first accepted that I had been sexually abused, and that I had a gambling problem. That acceptance is just the beginning of a long journey of healing and understanding.

An ADHD diagnosis is an invitation to people with the disorder to put down the tons of shame they have been carrying, and start to explore their lives through a lens of compassion rather than the narrative of personal failure and brokenness. It may sound counterintuitive, but Rox's ADHD became more prominent after her diagnosis. With the safety to be herself and unmask, the behaviours she had fought so long to suppress began to overflow into her life. This is a fundamental part of the healing journey for many late-diagnosed people. The aim of diagnosis isn't to eliminate ADHD or to turn the person into a productivity machine. Rather, the goal is to help the person integrate ADHD behaviours into their lives in a shame-free way. That's when the person blossoms. When they finally stop trying to fix what isn't broken and allow themselves to grow.

We aren't trying to stamp out ADHD behaviours; we are going to encourage them, understand them and support them.

An ADHDer who doubts that they actually have ADHD is telling you something about themselves. They are telling you that they believe they deserve to struggle alone, that they deserve to feel like bad people. On a deeper level, this is a person who has likely been fighting alone for so long to just keep their head above water that they don't know another way. They don't want to get on the lifeboat because they feel that kicking about in the water is where they are meant to be.

How to Help an ADHDer
Who Believes They're a Bad Person

A late-diagnosed ADHDer has spent their life trying to understand what is wrong with them, and trying to fix it. They will have made failed attempt after failed attempt at being neurotypical. Often, they have received no support, and what has been reflected back to them is judgment and their own personal failing. The only rational answer to explain their life and troubles was to believe they were bad to their very core.

The wounds left by believing you are bad include low self-esteem, not believing you are worthy of love, not chasing your dreams as you don't feel you deserve them, constantly apologising, and allowing yourself to be mistreated by people as you feel on some deep level you deserve to be punished. However, we live in an age where ADHD awareness is growing, and no other kid needs to grow up believing something is wrong with them.

Here are a few ways you can help someone with ADHD start to dismantle the belief that they don't deserve their diagnosis:

1. **USE SAFE COMMUNICATION**: Your ADHDer has likely been wearing many masks for a long time. Pretending to be okay. Pretending to get by. Forcing themselves into a neurotypical shape and blaming themselves when they don't fit. Opening up space for communication about how they truly feel about day-to-day struggles and wider life issues lets them start to truly unmask and be who they are on the inside. This will likely come with a fear of rejection and being judged, as that is all they have known. Lean into their stories with curiosity, not with judgment.

2. **BECOME AN ADVOCATE**: Educating yourself about ADHD can be incredibly helpful, not only for your own understanding but also in moments when your ADHDer may need reminding that this is a valid diagnosis for them. You can counterbalance that little voice inside their head that calls them a fraud or a fake by learning about the condition and its effects. In this way, you can help them build blocks of their own identity and quiet their doubts about not deserving it.

3. **BE AWARE OF ABUSIVE DYNAMICS**: People who believe they are fundamentally bad people will often remain in relationships that treat them as second-class citizens. There may be friends who take advantage of them, work colleagues who constantly judge and critique them, or, more painfully, family members who refuse to see their condition and offer help. Where appropriate, it can be very helpful to point these out to your loved one with ADHD. This isn't done with the intent of controlling them or telling them what to do. Rather, it should be phrased as a reflection of the dynamics you are witnessing. For instance, you could say, "I've noticed this person is demanding a lot of your time, and it seems to be causing you some anxiety. I'm here to chat it through if you'd like to."

4. **ASK BIG QUESTIONS**: We know that ADHDers aren't massive fans of small talk. So, asking the right questions, the deeper questions, can be an important exercise in understanding what is really going on. For example, if your ADHDer is questioning whether they deserve their diagnosis, it would be easy to say "Yeah, that makes sense," and leave it at that. But there is a beautiful opportunity here to explore the root cause of this question! Ask them why they feel they don't deserve it. Ask when they first believed they

were broken, or for how long they have been unsupported.
Often underneath the doubt that they actually have ADHD
is a person who has had to do life alone for a very long
time, believing that they are at fault for all their struggles.

Reframing the Lie

When they say this:
~~ADHD isn't real, I'm just a bad person.~~

Try telling them this:
You have ADHD.
You deserve not only your diagnosis, but also all of the support that
comes with it.

ADHD Lie #6: Everybody Secretly Hates Me

Written by Rox

I have a deep sense of personal unlikability. A sense that when I walk out of a room, people will start laughing. A sense that no matter how much I try to do the right thing, I will be singled out as getting it wrong. It doesn't matter if we've been friends for two decades, or married for years. I can easily believe that you secretly hate me.

When you believe you are deeply unlikable, you of course try to act in ways to stop people from disliking you. The best way to stop being unlikable? Become the most sickly sweet, nicest person you have ever met in your life. I developed strategies for this over the years, my own foolproof methods to ensure nobody would be able to secretly dislike me, because I would do absolutely nothing to give them cause to do so. Here was my recipe for being liked by everybody:

- Have zero needs whatsoever.
- Put everybody else before yourself (including strangers).
- Always say yes when asked for help.
- Offer help, even when it isn't asked for.
- Always pay the bill even if you put it on a credit card.
- Never challenge someone's behaviour even when it borders on abusive.
- Smile, always.

- Accept mistreatment with grace.
- Never defend yourself.
- And never complain about any of it.

I decided that being a super-nice person would keep me safe. That I'd be accepted, liked and conflict-free. So I made myself as small as possible. I took up zero space. I quietened my voice and allowed everybody else's needs to rule my life. I was simply a resource for others to use, hoping that their gratitude would mean a happy life.

The result wasn't in fact that I felt happy—rather, I felt resentful and used. And it was all my own doing. This disastrous approach wasn't just how I acted with friends and loved ones. It permeated every single area of my life . . . including work. Accepting the worst deals on the table. Never pushing back when being taken advantage of. Giving away far more than what was fair.

A rude fucking awakening awaits you when you realise that giving up all of your power to other people in the hopes they will decide to treat you fairly, actually ends in them taking advantage again, and again. When I tried to play nice with someone, it ended up with them walking all over me. My attempts at being liked by everybody meant I didn't like myself very much. I was in a cycle I like to call the "people-pleaser's conundrum."

The People-Pleaser's Conundrum

1. You give more than what is fair in order to be seen as nice.
2. The other side takes it willingly and more.
3. You don't get praised for being nice or fair; you merely get taken advantage of.
4. You begin to feel resentful.

5. You swallow it down and overextend yourself again.
6. Yet again, your efforts are swallowed up.
7. Your resentment begins to spill over and you speak up.
8. Your limits are met with rage and shock, as the taker is met with your boundaries for the first time.

It's a pretty toxic tango. It's like entering into an agreement with somebody without them even knowing. I will be sickly sweet to you and give you power over me, and in return you must treat me like a soft, squishy baby . . . Ha—the naivety!

I once read a funny tweet that went something like this: "The funny thing about people-pleasers is that no one around them actually seems pleased." It could not be truer in my case. My likeability plan never got me what I wanted, which was fair treatment from others. Rather, it got me a ten-ton sack of resentment that would spill over and end up poisoning the dynamic of a situation. If you are liked for your people-pleasing ways, you aren't really liked. You are just useful. A tool. A part of somebody else's plan. You never actually give people the chance to know the real you, the messy, human, sensitive one who also has needs. And when you feel hard done by that no one sees this part of you, even though you are the one hiding it, it often ends in a relationship breakdown with both sides feeling very misunderstood.

So why is it that so many people with ADHD end up being people-pleasers? 99 per cent of the time, the answer is RSD, which stands for "rejection sensitive dysphoria." It's a smart-sounding way of saying we are extremely effing sensitive and think everybody hates us, even when they don't. Here is a little more on RSD, and what might set it off:

RSD Triggers:

- **EXTERNAL**: Criticism or negative feedback from others. Being rejected or excluded. Failure and setbacks.
- **INTERNAL**: Negative self-talk. Perfectionism. Low self-esteem.
- **PERCEIVED**: Anticipation of rejection or criticism. Hypersensitivity to social cues. Fear of disappointing others.[11]

And here's an example from my own life of each of these triggers at work:

- **EXTERNAL**: Recently I was in a meeting to do with my music. Somebody said "I wonder what would happen if you wrote a happy song?" It was meant with genuine kindness and curiosity. It was friendly advice. But what I heard was "I hate all the songs you have written, do better." I started crying in a room of middle-aged men.
- **INTERNAL**: Before releasing my first EP, "Good Die Young," I had a massive freak out. Two weeks before release I decided it was the biggest pile of shit ever and wanted to throw away all the songs. I was embarrassed by the work and felt physically sick at the thought of people listening to it. Luckily, I was talked down off that particular cliff, and I'm happy to say I'm glad I released it and I'm proud of it. But when RSD hits everything gets warped.
- **PERCEIVED**: A couple of weeks ago I decided that one of my best friends actually hated me. She had sent a slightly shorter than normal text with no smileys, and that was all I needed to feel the familiar sickness and anxiety that

something was incredibly wrong. I did an absolutely *insane thing* and asked her if she was okay . . . turns out she was in a mad rush to get a train, hence the lack of emojis.

RSD will have us project the worst possible explanation onto every situation:

- Constructive criticism will feel like a deep-rooted personal attack.
- Our own creations can become the most repulsive thing in this world.
- And personal relationships can move very quickly to becoming unsafe.

When I was younger, I was in an emotionally abusive professional relationship for *five years*. It was with a person who had a lot of power over me, who would abuse this position by screaming at me, guilting me, lying to me, and stealing from me. In those years I lost a lot of myself, and it has taken a lot of therapy to rebuild myself from what he did to me. Looking back, one thing always baffled me, though: why did I stay so long? Why didn't I say anything? Why didn't I leave? I believe that RSD is the reason I stayed. I was so scared of speaking up for myself because it might bring about rejection, so I stayed silent. The deep people-pleasing dynamics I had developed over a lifetime of trying to be accepted, meant that I chose to smile and avert my eyes when somebody was making serious verbal threats to my face.

People with ADHD are more vulnerable to those types of relationships. We may find ourselves drawn to people who seem to have things together, who are confident, domineering, and potentially also very controlling. I wonder how big a part RSD plays in that—the deep sense of personal failure that causes so much pain we will do anything to fix it, including allowing ourselves to be mistreated. When you have spent so many years pretending you have no needs, trying to appease others around you, you're left with a crippling consequence: asking for what you want can feel selfish, and asserting yourself can feel like aggression.

My experience with my abuser was a learning curve—or, more accurately, a sharp learning *drop* off a 500-foot cliff. I realised that in order to stop this ever happening again, I would need to take my own power back. I'd need to stop trying so hard to be liked, especially by people with a penchant for screaming at me. But, of course, fundamental change like this doesn't happen overnight. And I find myself still playing out familiar patterns even now.

When I met Rich, I thought I was doing rather well with asserting myself. Nobody in my life was regularly shouting at me, and that felt like a massive win. Yet the feedback he often gave me was "You are being too nice." Whether it was overextending to make myself available for a friend, overworking on somebody else's project, or accepting the raw end of a deal at work, niceness was still getting in the way.

Seen through an RSD lens, I can see someone who was desperate to prove her worth, both at work and in relationships. Petrified that I would be rejected, I overextended myself constantly in an attempt to remain valuable to other people. I never rocked the boat. Any emotions or desires that rose up in me were squashed as quickly as they had poked their little heads above water! Personal needs were selfish, I admonished myself. That is not a route to being Miss Congeniality Worldwide.

Having RSD feels like your every move is being perceived by 1,000 pairs of judgmental eyes, waiting for you to mess up, to do something wrong, or, worse, to do something selfish. One of my greatest fears was being called selfish. Being perceived as somebody who put their own needs first, went after their own dreams, used their skills for their own satisfaction—all these felt deeply uncomfortable for me. At this point I was working as a songwriter for other people. It was pretty much a perfect job for a people-pleaser, really. You see, my job was to write songs other people would like and then release. I would be in the studio five days a week, working on ideas for other people. I knew I wanted to focus on my own artistic projects again, but it felt deeply selfish to do so, to abandon all these people who needed me to help them. To chase after my own dreams instead of working on other people's. In reality they didn't need me at all, this was just the narrative I was telling myself!

Here is the biggest and the most insidious problem with RSD and the sense that everybody dislikes you: it will force you to play small. To never have a dream of your own. To never achieve your own potential. To never go after your own dreams, whatever they may be. Putting yourself out there becomes a scary and fearful act because it invites judgment, criticism, and the chance that you may be disliked, not only by friends and family, but by strangers. You yourself may even wonder who the hell you think you are to believe you can chase your own dreams.

Eventually, in 2021, I did the unthinkable: I joined TikTok and started posting videos of songs I had written for myself. They began to go viral. What has followed in the last couple of years has been a blossoming of the thing I have always desperately wanted, but never thought I would achieve: to be an artist. To sing songs to people who feel a deep connection with them. I've released two EPs (yes, including the one I tried to throw away!) that I am immeasurably proud of. I have done a sold-out tour of the UK, and I now have a community of people with similar histories to mine coming together to share a collective pain. It has been the most wonderful and restorative experience.

Every step of the way I have felt embarrassed and ashamed. I was sure that friends and family were judging me. I didn't feel like my art was very good. I was convinced the majority of the internet hated me. And . . . I have done it anyway.

Time and time again, my worst instincts are proved incorrect. The shame never comes. The exclusion never comes. In fact, quite the opposite . . . Slowly but surely, I'm learning that when you put yourself out there, warts and all, for the world to see, people seem to like you more, not less. Authenticity trumps insecurity.

Of course, it doesn't matter how much positive feedback I get: the default setting is still unlikability. For instance, I will be performing at Download Festival in 2024 for the first time, one of the largest rock festivals in the UK. It's an honour to be included, and I am so grateful to my amazing team for getting me a slot there. But me being me, I am filled with visions of nobody showing up, or, worse, people holding up signs that say, "RØRY [the name of my artist project] IS SHIT." But I'm still going to show up. And I'm going to be open to the fact that all those fears I feel deep in my bones might not actually be the truth.

That's all we have to do: be open to being wrong. There is no quick fix for RSD. The best way through it is to know that we are prone to it, and to protect ourselves as best as possible when it rears its head. The truth is, people probably don't hate you. At least not everybody. And those who do aren't worth your time. We aren't supposed to be liked by everybody. We aren't pizza. (You're not into pizza? Chocolate, then!)

Here's my little RSD survival guide, with the on-brand acronym of N.I.C.E.:

1. **NOTICE**: When you feel triggered either by internal, external or perceived rejection, call out what is happening. "My RSD has been triggered." Just that is often enough to stop it escalating and will give a little sense of understanding and control to what is happening.

2. **INHALE**: Take a breather . . . literally! RSD can be emotionally overwhelming and we don't want to act when we are amped up. Practise deep breathing, go for a walk, anything you can do to calm your body down and find your calm.

3. **COMFORT**: We are going to be incredibly kind to ourselves. Offering nice words, calm space, and non-judgment. You can also seek comfort from a safe family member or friend.

4. **EXPLORE**: Revisit the trigger. What exactly was it that caused it? Are you adding a negative self-belief to this event? Could your RSD be preventing you from seeing what is really happening? Do you need to speak up and set a boundary? Do you need some advice? Take time to really unpack what happened from a calm place before moving forward.

RSD is often mentioned within our community as one of the worst symptoms of ADHD. It makes sense. Believing everybody in your life secretly hates you is a horrible way to live. You never get to fully relax and be yourself. But like everything else connected with ADHD, we aren't here to banish it but rather to work alongside it with kindness. There will be a reason why you developed RSD. My totally non-scientifically-proven theory is that perhaps rejection reminds us of traumatic times in our early lives when we were judged and rejected by our caregivers. Whatever the cause, though, we have to be aware of it so we don't play small. So we aren't fearful of becoming our best selves. And so we can accept love and deep friendship from those around us.

Unlearning the "Everybody Secretly Hates Me" Lie

RSD is present in almost 100 percent of people with ADHD. It is very likely to be affecting you deeply, perhaps without your even knowing it. The layers are extremely complex, kind of a "chicken or egg" dynamic. Does the inherent RSD mean we feel deeply unlikable from birth, or does living in a world with people who do not understand our needs and sensitivities cause RSD? The truth is, I don't know. What I do know is that it can have devastating consequences on important relationships, and on our ability to find safety in this world.

To live believing everyone hates you will inevitably mean you walk with your shoulders down. It means playing small and playing safe, hiding your magic to avoid ever being judged. But RSD doesn't have to win: we must rally against the negativity that swirls in our own brains, share our struggles with those closest to us, and take steps towards things that petrify us.

Over time, it isn't that RSD goes away, but that we learn to act in spite of it.

Here are a few things you can do to take the edge off RSD:

1. **IDENTIFY SAFE RELATIONSHIPS:** Not all relationships are worth saving, or worth being vulnerable in. Being vulnerable in an abusive space can lead to devastating and long-lasting effects. Safe people are those who do not shout, shame or manipulate. You will not feel like you owe them something, or like you are walking on eggshells around them. Instead, there will be a lightness, an openness about how you feel with them, like you could say or do

anything and still be liked. Those are the relationships to nurture.

2. **BE VULNERABLE**: Within the confines of a safe relationship, opening up and asking how someone feels about you is an incredibly healing thing to do. It allows the other person to see how dark your thoughts can get, and to offer you reassurance and love. It is also important that we do not act on our first impulse, the one that tells us to leave, to run, to block, to disconnect. Yes, these can be valuable tools if a relationship has become toxic, but the lens of RSD will not have us seeing clearly, especially if a triggering event has just happened. Take time to talk things through with loved ones. Use the N.I.C.E. technique described in this chapter. And choose your action when you are back in a calmer and more confident place.

3. **LEARN TO TOLERATE BEING DISLIKED**: One of the most important skills to have in your arsenal is the ability to tolerate being disliked. Rejection is inevitable—you can't be everyone's cup of tea, and inevitably you're going to upset someone or let them down. It's uncomfortable as hell to feel this, but it is absolutely necessary to learn to live with it if we are to stop the pattern of trying desperately to be liked by everyone. Some people are going to love you deeply and wildly forever. Some people will think you are just okay. And some will dislike you or maybe even hate you. But as the French author André Gide once said, "It is better to be hated for what you are than to be loved for what you are not."

4. **FEEL THE FEAR AND DO IT ANYWAY**: If you are scared that pursuing your dreams is going to end up with people hating you, then you are likely not showing up for yourself, or showing the world all you have to offer. It is not

a selfish act to want to share your story, your art, your voice. In fact, it is the opposite: it is selfless to bare your soul in whatever form brings you the most joy. It allows others to see who you truly are, and may give someone else the courage to do the same. Fear is so very often a road map to the thing we actually need to do.

Reframing the Lie

Instead of this:
~~Everybody secretly hates me.~~

Try this:
I trust the people I love to tell me if there is an issue.
I sometimes need extra reassurance, and that is okay.

"No, I'm Not Mad at You"

Written by Rich

"Babe," Rox said, "I've got something to tell you. I've treated myself to a birthday present."

It's 9:32 p.m. We are already in bed. This is the kind of rock 'n' roll behaviour you can expect from two sober people in their mid-thirties . . .

"Ah! I love that for you!" I tell her, leaning up on one elbow. "You deserve it. How much did you spend?"

"Nine thousand dollars."

All the air went out of me. This was back in 2021 when I was still helping Rox work her way out of a "very poor" credit rating. We had registered her to vote. Paid back some old debts. And put her name on the utilities. She was working to a budget each month and working incredibly hard to change her impulsive habits. So, when she dropped $9,000 on a birthday present, I was pretty surprised.

After a bit of investigative digging, what I actually found out was that Rox was spending $9,000 on a music video for her song "Uncomplicated." She had dressed it up as a birthday splurge because she thought I would be angry at her for organizing a music video.

So, here I will introduce you to a rather difficult dynamic that has happened often between me and Rox:

1. She would commit to something, perhaps an event or a big expenditure.
2. She would assume I would be angry about this and so not tell me.
3. The date would come closer and closer.
4. She would eventually have to tell me, as it was unavoidable that I would find out.
5. She would be an anxiety bomb, knowing she should have handled it differently.
6. I would be a bit frustrated, not because she had made a plan or spent money, but because she'd withheld it from me.

This dynamic has played out time and again between us: when she booked music videos, made plans for us to go and see friends, signed us up for gym classes, and a whole host of other things. Every time, she would have to come clean: the guilt of keeping her decision a secret would become too much, and she would be a total mess. Confused about why she hadn't just told me in the first place. Upset with herself because she knew that, had she told me earlier, things would have been absolutely fine.

Yet, here we were, in bed, *the night before* a music video shoot.

By contrast, when I plan something that both Rox and I are involved in, it's a pretty simple procedure for me.

"Babe," I'll ask her, "do you fancy dinner with Andy and Claire next Sunday?"

"Sure," Rox will say.

I am presented with an option. I ask her if she's in. We make a decision, and then it's done.

But with Rox, decisions seem to go through a much more complicated process. She will be asked to do something or decide to do something. She will likely commit to it out of impulsivity, and possibly a need to please the other person. She will then feel immense fear that I will be mad at her, and that in turn will cause her not to tell me. She will then tie herself in knots over the coming days or weeks, as she struggles to withhold this information, and the whole thing often ends in a last-minute shame-heavy confession.

The first few times this happened, it was really confusing to me. It felt like I was being misled, and lied to, which is something I find incredibly difficult. I just couldn't understand Rox's behaviour; it made no sense. I had never once been angry with her, raised my voice to her, or judged her for wanting to spend money on things or make social plans together.

Without a proper understanding of what was really going on, I think this pattern could have done some serious damage to the trust in our relationship. As is customary with self-fulfilling prophecies, by withholding things from me in an attempt not to annoy me, Rox *was* actually annoying me. The defense mechanism of avoiding anything she feared would rock the boat was backfiring.

When I first learned about RSD, it was like being given an instruction manual for Rox.

Someone might feel intense emotional pain for what they perceive as rejection by another.

The words struck home with me. When Rox did something she thought I might disapprove of, like agreeing to spend a large amount of money, she would feel extreme emotional pain, fearing that if I knew what she had done, I would reject her. That somehow my love for her was conditional and I was just waiting for her to mess up so I could be angry at her. It totally shifted my perspective on the pattern that was playing out.

What was needed, I realised, was a really honest conversation. And a rather large amount of reassurance from me that I would never scream at her, or reject her, or stop loving her because she had made dinner plans with friends and not told me. The relief on her face as I said these words out loud was palpable, like she had finally been let off a hook she had dangled herself on for years.

Rox has ADHD. She is constantly making plans, agreeing to arrangements, and spending money on things, sometimes impulsively. It is never meant with bad intent, and it always comes with a sense of "Oh, shit. I should have told Rich about that" afterwards. But the bottom line is she isn't intentionally trying to deceive me. She is just petrified of being hated.

So often it is easy to label someone as having bad intentions. As being manipulative, defensive or secretive. These are all words that come with a heavy load of shame and a sense of personal badness. Painting an ADHDer this way only adds to their already extremely low view of themselves, their pervasive sense that they are not valuable and don't deserve unconditional love.

These days, Rox makes an incredible effort to involve me in her impulsive decisions. Some, of course, slip through the net, like her decision to totally rewrite this book that we told you about in the Introduction! However, she feels safe to tell me when she has just told a friend we're meeting up, or booked in a music video shoot. But even now, after years together, and so many experiences of knowing that I would never harm her, or be angry with her, she still experiences enormous fear when she tells me certain things. It's as if she is waiting for the other shoe to drop. Very often, after she's shared something she is planning to do or told me her vision for something, she will quickly ask me, "Are you angry at me?"

Every time, I answer no. But that core wound within her that is waiting for me to turn on her at any moment is ever-present. The important thing is that she feels safe to ask. That's the end goal here. Not fixing the RSD; not trying to force it to go away. In my experience, that only makes her feel more judged and more likely to retreat back into avoiding things. Instead, we maintain a very safe, almost fun, open house where she can drop a "Do you hate me?" at any point and get reassurance. It has taken on an almost comedic feeling for us.

Another behaviour that I witnessed, one that impacted Rox in a hugely negative way, was overextending herself for others. Going to meet friends when she was burned out. Committing to extra days of work when she was behind on her own projects. Always being at the beck-and-call of certain friends who would abuse the fact that she made herself constantly available to them. You see, Rox wasn't just petrified of being hated by me. She was afraid of being hated by anyone at all. When someone asked Rox for her time, it was like she was driven by a motor. There was never a check-in with herself, her plans, or her wishes. It was just always, "Yes. I can help."

I remember one friend in particular would call her every day, often to vent about her latest drama, and almost always looking for reassurance from Rox. The phone calls were often hours long, and Rox would finish the call drained of energy and shattered. But when I pointed out that perhaps she didn't have to always answer the phone, she became defensive.

"But I have to be there. I have to be reliable. It's a good thing."

I realised that Rox wore her people-pleasing as an armour. Something to be proud of. But as time went on, her anxiety about these daily phone calls, and her resentment at the time she was giving to those conversations, got to be too much. She told her friend she wanted to speak a little less frequently, and this eventually resulted in the end of the friendship. You see, when someone is trapped in trying to be liked by everybody, they are a magnet for people who will use that, who will ultimately drain them of their energy. This dynamic isn't true friendship or connection; it's a power play. But through an RSD lens, someone with ADHD thinks they *have* to act this way to be accepted.

Things are different now. Rox assures me she doesn't have anyone in her life like that anymore. She has a few core friends, some wonderful support at work, and the three of us at home. But it has taken years for her to move away from being sucked dry by other people, and she still needs helpful reminders to check in with herself and to set boundaries.

An ADHDer's natural setting is to be consumed by others, but they must learn to protect themselves from these instincts so they can begin to unlock their own identity and potential.

How to Help an ADHDer Who Believes Everybody Secretly Hates Them

RSD is one of the most difficult struggles for ADHDers. It means they live under a constant cloud of belief that they are doing something wrong, and are about to be rejected. It can lead to people-pleasing, overextending themselves, and avoidance behaviours. Not to mention really difficult emotional triggers that can result in consequences they don't actually want.

Our job in supporting them is to create a safe space and provide reassurance. And it likely isn't enough to reassure them just once that you're not angry, or going to reject them. The RSD thought pattern is a constant in the ADHD brain—it is *always* there, reminding them they are not good enough and are disliked. So, our reassurance, at least in the beginning, must also be constant. It will take time for them to put their defenses down and show you how troublesome their thoughts are when it comes to other people. However, it is only by sharing these thoughts, and by being reassured, that those fears will begin to lessen and they will begin to build a newer, stronger inner voice.

Here is how to help someone with RSD:

1. **REMIND THEM THAT THE GOAL ISN'T TO BE LIKED BY EVERYONE**: Remind your ADHDer that it is impossible to be liked by everyone, and they will burn out trying to make that happen. Rather, it is important to be liked and loved by the safe people in their life, those whom they deeply value. Help them learn to take back their energy, to avoid spreading themselves too thin by trying to be liked by everyone, and show them how to invest that energy in their own lives and dreams, and in relationships that give back in return.

2. **HELP THEM CONNECT TO THEIR BODY**: Our bodies are highly intuitive. They can know when things aren't right, or if something is off with someone. But ADHDers have become masters at overriding these signals, due to their desperate need to be liked and stay safe. Helping them connect back to their body might look like pointing out that they appear particularly anxious or run down after spending time with certain people or on certain tasks. We want them to begin to connect the dots and realise that they can choose to fill their time with things that feel energy-giving and safe.

3. **BE REALLY HONEST**: ADHDers are incredibly sensitive and emotionally attuned. They are often very alert to other people's micro-expressions. However, the lens of RSD can magnify a tiny flash of annoyance on someone else's face to catastrophic proportions. If an ADHDer asks you if you hate them, and if in that moment, something has bothered you a little bit, share that with them. Don't pretend nothing is up. This helps them to learn two things:

first, that they can actually trust their gut instincts, and second, that someone can be a little upset or tired, but that doesn't mean the end of the relationship or total rejection.

4. **USE LOTS OF HUGS, CUDDLES AND AFFECTION**: Physical affection is a great stress-buster, and an awesome way to co-regulate. It's a way to make someone feel really safe. If your ADHDer is feeling sensitive, criticised or lonely, they may find it helpful to be cuddled or given some other type of physical affection. This can help them move through emotional triggers brought on by RSD and move to a calmer place where, often, they can access the more rational parts of their thinking.

Reframing the Lie

When they say this:

~~Everybody secretly hates me.~~

Try telling them this:
Not everybody is going to like you, and that's okay.
I really love you.

ADHD Lie #7: I Am Useless

Written by Rox

Sprinting down the stairs, I am filled with hope that I will in fact make my train. I have an appointment with the hairdresser in about an hour. I grab my bag and coat. Put my shoes on. Oh, shit. Where's my wallet? A hurried look in the obvious places:

> The bowl by the door where I had committed to always putting my wallet.
> Yesterday's coat pocket.
> The kitchen coffee table.
> It's nowhere to be seen.

My face starts to burn hot; the anxiety rises in my chest, I'm on the edge of breaking down in tears and punching a hole through the wall.

This is what I call "panic leaving." Let me introduce you to the concept. *Panic leaving* is when an ADHD person is leaving the house and realises they are missing a crucial item. Due to a desperate desire not to be late, this realisation leads to frantic searching and panic-like sensations.

Leaving the house in this manner is a pretty sure sign I'm going to have a terrible day. My body never fully recovers to feeling okay and regulated, meaning that, for the rest of the day, I am attempting to walk around like a normal person and conduct adult-like activities, with a brain full of fuzz and fear. A frantic morning creates a domino effect, leading to an often chaotic and stressful day.

Let me tell you about the next domino to fall . . .

I arrive at the train station and sprint to the ticket machine. Of course, I am unable to collect my ticket without my wallet. I dash to the ticket office to join a queue. Stood politely behind eight other customers, I watch the minutes tick by, knowing my train will be leaving soon. There is a supernatural belief in me, an eternal optimism that somehow this queue will move quickly, the train will be late, some act of God will allow me to make this train. Alas, no miracles today. I watch my train pull away, a sinking feeling in my stomach.

I text my hairdresser: *Hi Fede. I'm so sorry but I've missed my train. ADHD, lol. I'm going to be a little bit late for my hair appointment but I'll try and make up the time and be there as quick as I can!*

"I'll try and make up the time." This is the worst possible thing you can commit to when running late. A combination of stress in my body from the lost wallet, directional dyslexia, and the added pressure of promising to make up the time is a sure-fire way to ensure I will in fact make myself later than I currently am.

I know that stress makes ADHD symptoms worse.

I've written a book about it.

My full-time job is raising awareness of it.

My friendly advice from *Dirty Laundry*: "If you're feeling panicked, take a few moments to breathe deeply to help regulate yourself" feels like it was written by somebody else entirely. I shall not be taking a fucking break to breathe. I will be sprinting from point to point desperately trying to correct the error of my ways.

I board the next train. Currently, I'm running fifteen minutes late. Not so bad. I can make this up. But . . . I probably should calm down. I feel awful. I reach for my phone and noise-cancelling headphones. Time to tune the world out and get myself back together.

As I root through my bag, my stomach drops.

Where the hell are my headphones?

Not today. Please, not today.

I search my bag and pockets multiple times, hoping that in my panic I may have missed seeing them. I don't trust my own eyes, with good reason! I cannot tell you the number of times I have searched "thoroughly" for something in my bag, declared it missing, only for Rich to locate it with one fell swoop! Eventually, though, I have to accept the unacceptable. I am on a train to London, stressed out, and with no headphones.

The train noises. The random strangers talking loudly. And the cardinal sin: someone is eating crisps.

My blood begins to boil. My stress-riddled brain, desperately reaching for something to help me feel more regulated, comes up with the worst possible idea I could have had at that time:

I know: I'll get off at London Bridge. I'll quickly run to buy some new headphones, and then get back on the train to Farringdon. It will take five minutes.

All the evidence I have collected over my entire life is screaming at me that this will *not*, in fact, take five minutes. Yet, the eternal optimist within me wins the battle. It may be physically impossible, due to the laws of the universe and, you know, how time works. But I can do it.

I jump off the train at London Bridge and awkwardly walk-run to WHSmith.

"iPhone headphones, please."

"Which ones?"

"Umm . . . Not sure."

"Let me see your phone."

The nice young man checks my phone and tells me I need the new iPhone earphones. I pay $38 for the privilege, and with my purchase in hand, dart back to the train station. As I put my ticket into the barriers to get back through to the main station, it beeps at me. *Seek assistance.*

I stare at my ticket, and realise with horror I have bought a return ticket instead of a day-travel card. Essentially this means getting off the train early and trying to reboard is not allowed. I need a new ticket to get back into the station. I take out my phone and slam it onto the automatic reader. It beeps letting me know it has deducted a new fare via ApplePay. The shame of my mistake is mounting, and what I call the ADHD tax is feeling extremely unfair in this moment. And more than that . . . I am feeling utterly useless. A floundering fish of an adult that should not be allowed out in the world unsupervised.

I make peace with the $13 I've just lost on a new ticket, reboard my train, and begin to feel a little bit calmer. Like a feral beast, I unbox my new headphones and go to plug them into my phone. I am seconds away from peace. Something about music, or even a podcast, helps me find myself in the chaos.

The adaptor doesn't fit.

Is it me? Am I being stupid?

I try shoving it in every which way.

Nope . . . I've been sold the wrong headphones.

A flashback to WHSmith . . . "No, I don't need a receipt, thank you."

That's it. That's the straw that broke the ADHD camel's back. I can't hold back my disappointment in myself any longer. I burst out crying, swamped by a tsunami of shame and embarrassment. I hate myself in this moment. A useless lump of human flesh, completely incapable of even the basic tenets of human functioning. I curse my horrible, stupid brain. If it lived outside of my body, I'd have happily given it a cold, hard kick.

My train pulls up to Farringdon. I'm now running twenty-five minutes late, and I'm resigned to the fact no miracle will be happening today. I just need to get to my hair appointment. I look for the exit signs. I can't see them. I follow the flow of people, and soon I'm stood on another platform. I'm lost. I feel trapped. I've had enough. I'm sweating. I feel sick. And I feel totally inadequate. I consider calling Rich. I know he'd help calm me down. But I feel so stupid in this moment that I don't even want to have to tell him that I'm lost in a train station.

I finally find a quiet corner on the platform and decide to take a few deep breaths. *Alright. I'll follow my own stupid fucking advice.* In the middle of an ADHD-induced panic state, the need for a breather will whisper to you, then ask quietly, and then finally scream until you take notice. I close my eyes and breathe in deeply for a count of eight, and then out again. I look up, and 50 metres down the platform a "way out" sign appears where I swear it wasn't just a few moments ago. I walk steadily towards it. Sweat begins pouring down my face. My panic has reached a critical level.

Holding back tears, I exit the station and walk towards the salon. Stifling the strong emotions, I realise I am not okay. I'm on the edge of a meltdown. I need to sit down. I need to take my coat off. I need to breathe, and probably to cry. I walk into a hotel bar—perfect, because it's pretty empty—order a cold Diet Coke, and find a seat hidden away in the corner. I fire off another text.

Fede, I'm so sorry. I've had the morning from hell. I am just having a quick drink and calming down and I'll be with you.

Luckily for me, Fede, my hairdresser, also has ADHD. I don't feel ashamed telling him what's happening, and I know there'll be no judgment. From our first appointment, he made it clear his salon is a mask-free zone. That being said, there is always a little RSD-tinged voice in my head telling me that he will secretly hate me and not want to dye my hair again!

After about twenty minutes, my body returns to a calm state for the first time in the day. My breathing is normal. I'm not as hot. I don't feel on the borderline of a panic attack. I feel okay—and can actually begin to look at my disaster of a day with a bit of shock, and a tinge of comedy. How have I survived thirty-nine years on this earth?!

That day, I was a walking checklist of ADHD symptoms and how they manifest:

- **Short-term memory loss**: My misplaced wallet.
- **Time blindness**: Believing I would make it.
- **Emotional dysregulation**: Panic attack-like symptoms when things began to go wrong.
- **ADHD tax**: Needing new headphones and a new ticket.
- **Directional dyslexia**: Getting lost in a station.
- **Rejection sensitivity**: Feeling like I would be hated for my tardiness.

This type of high-scoring day isn't a daily occurrence, thank God! But it does happen more regularly than I would like. It leaves me feeling like I don't belong, like I am utterly and disgustingly useless. Days like this always remind me why I much prefer to travel with Rich. I feel so lucky to have him, but also so ashamed of myself that I need that . . .

On my good days, I know I am not useless. I know that my strengths are creativity, empathy and divergent thinking. I know I struggle with misplacing things, directions and making simple mistakes. I try and give myself grace in those moments, and I try to move on. But when ADHD comes for your throat . . . At those times, despite knowing all of this, I am at its mercy. All of my failings are amplified in front of my eyes. I am at the court of Terrible Humans being tried for the crime of being Utterly Useless.

The evidence stacks up in front of me:

- ☑ Loses everything all of the time
- ☑ Never learns

- ☑ Can't keep her room clean
- ☑ Can't text her friends back
- ☑ Makes promises and breaks them all the time
- ☑ Quits everything
- ☑ Is oversensitive
- ☑ Is a burden to everyone
- ☑ Always gets it wrong
- ☑ Can't follow simple instructions

The jury, made up of my old boss, some old schoolteachers, and a few anonymous online users, are shaking their heads at me in disgust. My shoulders are slumped and there are tears in my eyes. I plead guilty to the crimes I've been charged with and await my sentencing . . .

BUT WAIT.

This isn't fair.

All these things you are accusing me of doing on purpose I am doing because of ADHD.

I have issues with executive function.

It's not my fault.

I am actually trying really hard.

I can also write a pretty awesome song!

I can also make resin coasters.

And I know loads about some really niche topics.

I've helped my partner and step-kids connect more to their emotions.

I'm not a great texter, but I'm great in person!

I'm on my feet now. Overcome with the desire to defend myself against judge and jury.

How about I put *you* on trial for your lack of creativity, special interests, and empathy? How about I roll my eyes at *you* when you can't write a book, or start a creative business, or immediately know what is going on under the stoic expression of a loved one? It wouldn't be fair, would it? To judge you as a failure because you don't possess the same skills as me?

Let's leave my imaginary courtroom for a second. I want to hammer something home for you.

If you have ADHD, you will struggle with things many others find easy.

And others will struggle with things *you* find easy.

Us ADHDers are going to have days where everything falls apart. Where everything goes wrong. And we feel like the most useless blob of human flesh to ever walk this planet. We have to move through it as best we can, and get back to the things that really matter.

When I got back from my ADHD horror day, I felt awful. I had a cuddle with Rich and went to bed extremely grumpy. The next day, I woke up, went to my little home office and began writing a chapter of this book—the one you are reading right now. Had I allowed the useless lie to really take hold, that would have felt impossible. I would not have felt capable or deserving of working on something creative and that I loved.

Lost headphones, missed trains, late appointments . . . they are all incredibly frustrating (not to mention, expensive!). But they do not have to define us. Being unable to function like a "normal" adult can absolutely obliterate our self-esteem . . . with the "useless" narrative poisoning all that we do. Our self-esteem is never going to come from being the most organized, from never forgetting something, or from having a perfectly kept home. That is, in fact, where our self-loathing is likely to come from! Our self-esteem will come from other areas! Places where we are anything but useless . . . Our empathy. Creativity. Big-picture thinking. Whatever your particular gift is, that is the thing to double-down on.

Unlearning the "I Am Useless" Lie

A lifetime of struggling with simple tasks, repeated mistakes, memory issues and emotional dysregulation does a number on us and our sense of self. Our constant failure after trying our absolute hardest leads us to conclude we are of no value. We are inept. We are bad adults. We are useless.

You are not useless for having a neurodevelopmental condition. You just have it. You have the symptoms of it. And you will sometimes struggle because of it. You deserve help and support with your struggles. You do not need an inner bully screaming at you because of it, denying you the opportunity to dream, to build something, to love a hobby, or to take a chance because you didn't memorise the rules of the National Rail booking system. You are not undeserving of a happy life because of ADHD. You have a lot to offer, whether that be in your own family or the wider community. We are wonky, and wonderful.

Here are some tips for beating the "useless monster."

1. **DON'T DEFINE YOURSELF BY BASIC SKILLS:** Your worth as a human does not depend on your ability to not get lost in a train station, or to never misplace your keys. Those things are not moral failings. They are just

a side effect of having ADHD. Annoying. Frustrating. But by no means does it mean you don't deserve a really happy and fulfilling life. Judge your life by your victories. By your heart, your love, your kindness, your creativity, your purpose.

2. **BE YOUR OWN CHEERLEADER**: When you find your inner voice telling you that you are useless because you've forgotten a birthday, or are having a meltdown due to the pieces of your Ikea flatpack furniture not quite coming together, speak back. Defend yourself as though you're speaking to a bully. This voice in your head is not who you are. It is the internalisation of the words and actions of those around you when you were developing. By speaking back, we begin to act as if we are worthy of respect, understanding and kindness.

3. **ADOPT A "SO WHAT?" PHILOSOPHY**: I'm bad at texting. I get lost easily. I lose things. So what? Seriously. So what? There are way worse things a person can do than accidentally cause a bit of havoc for themselves. Accept the fact that ADHD hurdles are going to be part of your daily life, and get back to business as soon as you can. Don't let symptoms derail an entire day—and on a bigger level, an entire identity!

4. **FIND YOUR GIFTS**: To counter the belief that we are useless, we want to find areas of life where we can excel, add value, and find true enjoyment. Self-esteem is built by doing hard things. By taking risks. By believing in ourselves. Trying new things. And overcoming problems. What if all the energy you spent on desperately trying to fix yourself was spent on trying to nurture your natural gifts? This world needs different perspectives, divergent thinkers, pattern seekers, daydreamers, highly sensitive people. We see the

world differently, and are capable of creating ideas, plans and solutions within our own minds. Find your magic. And allow that to be how you define yourself.

Reframing the Lie

Instead of this:
~~I am useless.~~

Try this:
I do have different struggles and I deserve support.
I have so many amazing things I excel at.

"You're Not Useless"

Written by Rich

"Can you believe I'm ready this early?!"

I look up to see that Rox is showered, dressed and raring to go. It's a miracle. We're on the way to a business meeting to meet a potential manager. He's invited us to go and see *The Nightmare Before Christmas*. Okay . . . so it's less of a meeting, and more just a really fun night.

We leave the house and drive to the station. We purchase our tickets and we're on the platform in good time. The train pulls in, on schedule and empty. The perfect combination. One change at London Bridge and we're on the way to the O2 Arena.

Rox and I don't really go out much. We're both sober and, as it turns out, pretty introverted. We're often in pyjamas and in bed before 9:30 p.m. So, it's pretty exciting to actually be venturing out! Especially for my favourite kind of event: something that's free!

We head straight to the Guest List VIP entrance, feeling a little bit awkward as we cut past a queue of people. But we can't complain. It's quieter than normal, and Christmas spirit is in the air.

"Hi, mate," I tell the box office man. "We have two tickets reserved under the name Mark Walker."

"Which show are you here for?"

"The Nightmare Before Christmas."

"Sorry, sir. That isn't showing here tonight."

If the walk to the box office was awkward, the walk away from it is even worse. Rox's expression is utterly bemused; she has no idea what's going on.

"Show me the confirmation, babe," I say to her.

She hands me her phone in a daze. There it is. Clear as day.

Two tickets.

Nightmare Before Christmas.

December 13th.

OVO Arena, Wembley.

We were at the O2 Arena in Canary Wharf. The other side of London. Forty-five minutes at the very best.

I see Rox's face fall in disbelief. The shame of getting the details wrong. Of ruining our night. Of wasting time. Of letting down the person we were meeting.

"I am so useless," she whispers. "I'm so sorry."

It's the start of a shame spiral, and there's not much I can do to stop it. We go to get a hot chocolate with marshmallows for a little dopamine hit, and to let Mark know what's happened.

"It sounds so stupid he won't even believe me. That's how idiotic I am," Rox says. "Mistakes so bad people wouldn't even use them as an excuse."

I'd like to introduce you to the concept of the "two arrows." The first arrow is when something goes wrong in life. The second arrow is the decision to speak to ourselves in awful ways.

Here's how it was playing out right in front of me:

The first arrow was realising we had come to the wrong place, wasted our trip, and let somebody down.

The second arrow was Rox calling herself useless, stupid, and a whole host of other names. Kicking herself when she was already down.

The first arrow is unavoidable for every single one of us. We all make mistakes, have bad luck, and have horrible things happen. For

ADHDers though, there's about ten times as many of those arrows flying around.

The second arrow is a choice. It doesn't have to be fired. The first arrow is enough pain. We don't need to destroy ourselves emotionally by launching the second one.

Moments like this are frequent in our house, where an ADHD arrow is fired into the middle of our life.

Here are some of our more memorable ADHD arrows:

- When Rox set the microwave on fire because she had put something in that had metal on it
- When Rox lost her eighth wallet
- When Rox lost her eighteenth pair of headphones
- When Rox spilled water over her brand-new laptop
- When Rox spent months planning presents for a surprise birthday for me and forgot to actually order them
- When Rox knocked her coffee all over the freshly painted white wall of our bedroom
- When Rox fell down the stairs because she was running late

The impact of these things is always nasty. There's often frustration, shock, and upset at the consequences of what has happened. That is difficult enough. This is not the time for Rox's nasty inner bully to pipe up and start making her feel even worse.

When we were first together, long before therapy, and long before her diagnosis, we went through what I like to call a bonding experience. Rox had moved into my flat. She'd immediately begun decorating and making it more homely, filling it with candles, cushions and pictures of the kids. It was so nice to have someone to help me make it more homely.

I noticed early on, however, that cleaning wasn't exactly Rox's strong suit, but she was trying exceptionally hard. Every day when I came home from work, I could see her tidy piles left all over the flat. Kitchen cleaner smeared on the taps and mirrors. Looking back now, I can see how hard she was masking, trying not to let me see how difficult she found this kind of work.

On one particular occasion, however, her mask slipped in a big way.

I looked at my phone and saw three missed calls in a row from Rox.

My heart skipped a beat. Something must be wrong.

A fourth call came in and I answered it with hands-free.

"What's up, babe?"

"I've flooded the kitchen! I don't know what to do. I can't stop it."

"Okay. Take a deep breath. What's happened?"

"I put a load in the dishwasher, but there were no tablets so I put washing-up liquid in, and now it's all foaming out of the machine."

"Press the big red button on the right of the stove," I told her. "This will turn the machine off. I'm home in twenty minutes."

I came home to find her shell-shocked, sat on the kitchen floor, staring at the mountain of bubbles in front of her.

"I'm so fucking useless. I've ruined everything. I'm so sorry."

It was the first time we had been ADHDed in a big way since we'd been together. Seeing my kitchen in such a state, especially as I love to keep a very tidy home, was pretty shocking and frustrating. But witnessing her on the floor in absolute pieces made something very clear. She hadn't done it on purpose. She was in a lot of distress. And it was more important to help put her back together than it was to wipe the bubbles off the floor.

A cuddle, a few kind words, and then a few jokes later, she was calm and able to laugh about the situation.

"I don't understand why you didn't scream at me," she said. "Or just break up with me."

Here's why her mind went there: Most ADHDers have been blamed their whole life for mistakes that are not their fault. They have been genuinely trying their best at any given task, then have made a very simple mistake and been punished for it. That punishment might be being hit, screamed at, laughed at, mocked, shamed or given the silent treatment. That rejection taught them the following lesson:

If I make a mistake, I am no longer deserving of love.

Years and years of making these mistakes, and being punished for it, leads to a deep sense of personal failure. And of being "useless." Unable to live like other adults. Overwhelmed by the simplest of things. Constantly feeling behind, and broken. It's a brutal way to live.

Floors can be mopped in about ten minutes.

Rebuilding self-esteem after years, often decades, of mistreatment? It's going to take a little longer.

I want to be really clear. I am not saying that flooding a kitchen, or setting a microwave on fire, or losing your keys twenty times are good things. They're stressful, and we should try and prevent them from happening. What I'm saying is that the moment when your ADHDer makes an innocent mistake is not the time to pile in with judgment and eye-rolls. They have't made these mistakes on purpose. In fact, they've been trying their damned hardest to try and be perfect.

We have adopted a Murphy's Law mentality in our house. Here's how it works:

- Anything that can go wrong, will go wrong.
- Ask for help if you're unsure.
- Plan thoroughly.
- Avoid guesstimates.
- Double-check things—or triple-check, if you can.
- Have a back-up plan.

Here are a couple of examples of how we use it in our house.

A) Murphy's Law dictates that Rox is going to lose her keys. To plan for it:

- I have a spare set, and the neighbours have a spare set.
- We've removed the fob from her key, which is harder and more expensive to replace.
- We have a spare already cut so she can be back up and running ASAP.

B) Rox is more likely than others to cause a house fire.

To plan for it:

- We do a candle check every time we leave the house.
- Rox asks us to triple-check labels before putting anything in the microwave.
- If Rox thinks she left her hair straighteners on, we go back to check.

The Murphy's Law mentality acknowledges that certain situations are likely to arise, and removes all pressure to be perfect. It allows Rox's struggles to be validated in a totally non-shaming way. I think Rox would still say she is pretty useless with remembering keys, remembering laundry in the dryer, and staying on top of finances. But there is a huge difference between "I am useless at remembering laundry" and "I am useless as a person."

The first statement is action based. It's located outside the self. It's isolated. It makes sense.

The second one is identity based. It affects overall self-esteem and self-belief.

I'm useless at playing guitar, decorating hallways, and reading, as it turns out. But I'm not a useless person. Look for the difference in your own life, and make sure you are not taking on uselessness as an identity.

How to Help an ADHDer
Who Believes They're Useless

It's very easy for someone's struggles to become their identity. Dealing with constant failures and criticisms. The sense of falling behind peers. Being unable to execute simple adult tasks. A constant state of overwhelm with the demands of life. When you add this together with no support, you get a person who feels totally unworthy and useless.

Your ADHDer may know their struggles are related to their condition but still struggle to let themselves off the hook. They are absolute pros at self-loathing. Allowing their struggles to be accepted and supported is a game-changer. With acceptance and support, there is no need to try harder, to make promises that will be broken, or to set themselves up to fail over and over. Mistakes will happen. Washing will be shrunk. Keys will be lost. It's not the end of the world. When they live in an environment that doesn't expect them to function like a neurotypical person, they can come out from under that heavy burden, and find all of the ways they are actually pretty incredible.

Here are some ways to help your ADHDer stop feeling useless:

1. **LOOK OUT FOR THE SECOND ARROW**:
   Mistakes will happen—those annoying first arrows. It's normal to be frustrated and upset when they hit. Where you can help your ADHDer is pointing out the second arrow: the nasty comments about self, the inner bully. That doesn't need to be there. Helping them with seeing how often they are mean to themselves and encouraging a different response will help to stop the constant torrent of negativity they have been living with.

2. **SHARE YOUR OWN STRUGGLES**: Your ADHDer may not have the same skill set as a neurotypical person. But they will have amazing skills in other areas. For example, Rox plays guitar. I can't. But I don't sit and shame myself for being useless at music. It just is what it is and it's okay. I have other skills deserving of the same grace most people walk around with. Where skills are celebrated, and struggles are accepted. Sharing things you find difficult, especially if these are things they are great at, will model how it's human to not be great at everything. And it will underscore that self-esteem doesn't need to be tied to any particular skill.

3. **BE AWARE OF LONGER BRAIN MATURATION TIME**: ADHDers' frontal lobes develop at a slower rate than neurotypicals, often not reaching maturity until they're 35 or 40, whereas neurotypicals' frontal lobes often reach this stage by 25. If your ADHDer is feeling like they're behind in life, they may simply be on a different developmental timeline.

4. **ACCEPT THAT THEY'RE DIFFERENT**: ADHDers often live with a sense of an ideal adult in their mind. One that is organized, great at admin and bills, keeping fit, eating well, and extremely tidy. It's a perfectionistic image that they use to beat themselves up with. Very often, this mythical perfect adult takes on the qualities of one or both of their parents, especially if those parents had skill sets that the ADHDer doesn't. It can be incredibly healing to ask your ADHDer if their parents lacked any skills, particularly in fields like empathy, kindness, emotional maturity, and creativity. They will be able to see that this "ideal" adult they have created isn't quite so perfect after all. There are different ways to adult, and the ADHD way is just as valid as any other way.

Reframing the Lie

When they say this:

~~I am useless.~~

Try telling them this:

Your ADHD symptoms aren't a personal failing.

You deserve support, not judgment.

ADHD Lie #8: I Am a Burden

Written by Rox

"Mummy . . . I left my teddy in the park." My voice began to wobble as fear started taking over 6-year-old Rox's body. The tears started to flow. Sadness. Grief. The thought of Betty, the cuddly toy that had been with me since I was born, left alone somewhere in a park in Southampton.

The silent annoyance of my father was palpable. An eye-roll. A shake of the head. And then the decision to drive fifteen minutes back to the park to get Betty.

"Isn't that lovely of him, going back to get your teddy?" my mother said as she cuddled me. I wonder now who she was trying to convince of my dad's loveliness—me, or her. I didn't know it at the time, but my parents had a very strained marriage. Sometimes I wonder why they stayed together. Perhaps it was because my mum always chose to see the best in my dad, to hold on to faith that he would change. That love would win in the end.

My 6-year-old mind, without any of this knowledge, absorbed the message: someone who shakes their head, tuts, is angry at you, but then decides to help you anyway is lovely. That is what kindness looks like. That is the best treatment I can hope for.

And I also learned this: *I am a burden.* My needs are an inconvenience to others. They have no obligation to help me, but if they choose to, in whatever capacity, I must be extremely grateful.

"Thank you so much, Daddy!" I squealed with excitement when Betty was returned to my hands.

It's funny . . . all these years later, eye-rolling and huffing have a very big effect on me. Early in my and Rich's relationship, he was to find that out the hard way! I was working hard on keeping my wear-again shelf tidy. It's a shelf in our bedroom where I put clothes that aren't ready for washing, but that it doesn't make sense to hang back up. We came up with the idea to try and keep the bedroom floor a bit clearer! And on the whole, it was working very well.

One evening, though, I got back late from work and forgot to use it. Instead, I deposited my clothes, sports bra and underwear on the floor next to my bed.

The following morning, Rich was putting on a load of washing. He noticed the clothes on the floor. Something I had promised not to do.

He did an eye-roll, a little shake of the head, as he bent down to pick them up.

I translated his small actions into the following:

You fucking idiot. Why can't you get it right? I've had enough of you.

There they were again. The tears. At 37 years old, a simple eye-roll had reduced me to a helpless child. Rich's demeanour and language changed instantly.

"Bubby . . . what's wrong?"

"It's the eye-roll. I know you don't mean it to be so bad, but it hurts so much. I feel so stupid. I'm sorry I forgot." Tears and snot were covering my face, a vision of beauty and grace . . .

"I'm so sorry . . . I was a bit frustrated at the clothes, but it's never okay to take that out on you. I'm sorry, and I'll really try not to eye-roll."

Can I get a "Hallelujah" for this man? Seriously? Because who acts like that? I often read comments online from people asking me where they can find someone like Rich. It always makes me smile. When we met, Rich was in active addiction. He had a ton of unprocessed trauma, and none of the incredible communication skills he has now. He had to work for it. He had to get sober. Get therapy. And work every day to become the incredible man, partner and father he is today. So, I found him where you find anyone: trying their best to survive as only they know how, in an often-cruel world. That's where we found each other.

Research has shown that the average person with ADHD receives 20,000 pieces of negative or critical feedback before the age of 10. That works out to five a day. The eye-rolls. The tuts. The blame. The frustration. We literally grow up in a hostile environment, without the support or understanding that we need to flourish. So, we find our own ways to cope with the devastating reality that we are disliked and merely tolerated by the people we are most desperate to be loved by.

I sometimes wonder whether rejection sensitive dysphoria, or RSD (which we discussed in Chapter 6) is actually related to our younger years, when we would receive criticism with no way to defend or explain ourselves. All the blows that we just had to take. All of the rejection and anger that we absorbed due to simply not acting like the adults thought we were supposed to act. Perhaps our sensitivity to criticism now is a traumatic response to all of that. Either way, as children with no way of understanding what is happening, all we can do is to try and protect ourselves from the criticisms that hurt us the most.

ADHD children are extremely sensitive. It's part of the beauty of ADHD. These sensitivities are both physical and emotional. We may struggle with bright lights, overwhelming noises, and people eating crisps on the train. We also may be able to feel the emotions of a room, interpret body language and know what someone feels without them having to say a word. It's a blessing and a curse. Without my sensitivity, there is no way I could be the partner I am to Rich or the step-mum I am to my kids. Or the songwriter I am. Or the author I am. All of these things really depend on using my deep aptitude for feelings. But I grew up in a house that despised feelings. Feelings were the enemy. Feelings betrayed us. Made us weak. And, perhaps more aptly, big feelings meant adults had to face things in themselves they weren't ready to face.

I learned from a young age how not to feel, or take up too much space. Dissociation, masking, alcohol. By the time I was 14 years old, I didn't cry in front of anyone. I didn't even cry at my mum's funeral. The sensitive part of me had been so mishandled, and so undervalued, that I had learned to hide it away. I mocked and laughed at "feelings people." I had fully assimilated the personality of my father.

But you can't outrun feelings. They are always there. And if they aren't expressed healthily, they will bubble over at the most inappropriate times. For me, this was when I was extremely drunk. I cannot tell you the number of times I was wasted in the presence of my dad and my step-mum when *bang!* Suddenly I'd be screaming and crying, bringing up things from the past that, for me, were still raw and traumatic, and, for them, were things they never wanted spoken of. When feelings come out mixed with eight cans of cider and a bottle of Prosecco, they do not come out in the ideal way. Unfortunately, this only leads to further shame.

For years and years, I lived totally repressed, other than the occasional emotional breakdown when I was drunk. I was the embodiment of a "problem child." Everyone got to feel like they had their shit together around me. And they all had someone to blame for the dysfunction in the family. If there was an issue, no doubt I was the cause of it. Family scapegoating, a term I have learned in recent years, is an incredibly painful experience. It is a silent abuse of sorts, where one child or adult in a dysfunctional family system is singled out as the cause of all problems. (I wonder if this happens to ADHD kids more often than to typical kids.) The role of the scapegoat in a family is to absorb all of the unprocessed emotions of the adults. If they can label you as defective, dramatic or problematic, then they never have to look inwards. In my family, then, I was used as a shield against the shame my dad and stepmother refused to feel.

Things are different now. Three years of intense psychotherapy taught me about the family I grew up in. Why the adults saw me as the problem. And how to break free of those destructive narratives. It also taught me how to cry. It sounds ridiculous, but truly that was my experience. I remember the first time I became emotional in therapy. Daggers in my throat, like swallowing glass, as my body tried to fight back the feeling.

"Lean into it," my therapist said calmly.

"I can't!" I said, and then burst into tears.

I now cry *all* the time—I'm talking three or four times a week. Even more when I'm premenstrual. I cry when I'm happy. I cry randomly because of the love I have for my step-kids. I cry because I miss my mum. I cry when I lose my wallet. I cry because I don't speak to my dad. I cry when I receive an email written in what I think is a slightly mean tone. I've cried numerous times while writing this book. It's just dawned on me there's going to be an audio version where I read it out loud, and I'll probably blub my way through that too. Ah well . . . emotions are healthy apparently . . .

Rich has been on this journey with me, and there's no way I could be as open and connected to my sensitivity without him. He has encouraged the crying, is always there with a co-regulating cuddle and a back rub, and afterwards he always has some kind words. But as I began my journey of learning how to cry as a 36-year-old woman, I would still experience severe shame.

My throat would tighten up, trying to restrict the emotion.

I'd feel small and helpless and scared.

I'd say "I'm so sorry."

One sure way to know that your sensitivity has been injured in some way is that you apologise for your tears. They are nothing to be sorry for. They are a beautiful, natural, human expression of deep feelings. A healthy release. I'm telling this to myself as much as to you by the way, because when the tears have stopped, I always get that familiar sharp pang of feeling like a burden.

The thing is, though, it isn't only crying that makes me feel like that. It is the constant, unrelenting mistakes that I make every day of my life:

A wallet left in a shop.

A meltdown due to a room being too loud.

Asking for the subtitles to be on.

Having to go home to get my headphones.

The bad credit rating from years of impulse spending.

A forgotten meeting I'm rushing to get to.

A wear-again shelf I've forgotten to use.

Clothes strewn on the floor.

Dirty dishes in the sink.

Cupboards of gear for hobbies that I no longer use.

Forgotten promises.

Forgotten birthdays.

Reading this list, it's hard to say I'm not a burden to Rich. I mean . . . I must be, right? All the emotional support he has to give me. The unpaid labour he takes on in our house. The finances and the admin that he has to take care of.

Here is one dictionary definition of the noun "burden":

Someone or something that is very difficult to accept, do, or deal with.

I know that I am accepted by Rich. He laughs about knowing me so well. Knowing when I'll forget something. Be late. Or drag us somewhere impulsively.

He also knows exactly how to deal with me. Kind little reminders. Emotional safety. Lower expectations.

So why is it so hard for me to accept that I am *not* a burden?

I suppose perhaps it's been one of my longest-held and most harmful beliefs. A thought habit I have practised over and over again. The belief that I am intolerable. That I need too much. That I am too sensitive. That I bring too many problems. That I need to change or else people will leave. I simply cannot fathom that he stays. That he puts up with me. Despite all evidence to the contrary, I expect his patience and kindness to eventually run out one day. How sad is that?

The truth is, in a healthy family system, or relationship, everybody will have needs that will be expressed and supported. Where I may need a regulation cuddle after a lost wallet or a bit of help replying to that one text, Rich will need my help to process his emotions, make decisions about how we parent the kids, and what creative challenge we'll be taking on next! It's not a zero-sum game whereby the amount of help we receive is only proportional to the amount we give. It's just a beautiful flow where everybody supports each other when it's needed.

Unlearning the "I Am a Burden" Lie

ADHD means you will need support, as well as extra time and care, in order to flourish. You have needs that other people don't. But having needs, and having a condition, does not make you a burden. Rather, we end up feeling like burdens when our behaviour has been seen as inconvenient from an early age. As we've absorbed the eye-rolls, the admonishments to "just focus," and the judgments of others.

We carry around an identity that was built on the premise that we are too much. Too needy. That we need to manage our own symptoms privately and not bother other people with our dramatic little problems. It's one of the worst ADHD lies, because it leaves you isolated and embarrassed to ask for help—and not knowing how to do that.

Let's kick burden-itis in the ass, shall we?

1. **LOOK AT THE ROOT CAUSE**: What is your earliest memory of feeling like a burden? Can you recall it? Can you see how you were treated unkindly or unfairly? Can you see how you would do things differently if you were your own loving parent? Understanding where this belief took root can help us to gain perspective on it and begin to challenge it as an infallible truth. We know now that our caretakers didn't understand we had ADHD and were instead interpreting our behaviour as being done on purpose. Often their only response was to shout, shame and punish. We will carry these wounds with us until we are brave enough to face them head on.

2. **KNOW THAT HAVING NEEDS IS HUMAN**: We have extra support needs when we have ADHD, whether it's for emotional regulation, organization, administration, anxiety reduction, or financial planning. We struggle in a lot of areas, often due to executive dysfunction. But that's absolutely okay. We can have needs, and still be absolutely loved, not resented. Healthy relationships are two-way streets in which support is given freely and lovingly where people need it most. Remember, you will be providing so much support to those you love as well!

3. **DON'T STAY WHERE YOU ARE MERELY TOLERATED**: It's easy to accept poor treatment when you hold this negative core belief that you're a burden. To allow parents, or bosses, or partners, to repeat the negative words and actions we grew up with. To let them eye-roll, complain, and in general just reflect that we are in fact burdensome and they are doing us a favour by tolerating us. You must protect yourself from these people. Do not stay

somewhere where someone repeatedly makes you feel like a broken or horrible person. That being said, people can change if they want to. And just because someone has judged you in the past doesn't mean they can't learn and change. But it is down to them to choose; it's not something we can force.

4. **SEEK UNCONDITIONAL LOVE**: Love doesn't run out. It doesn't have a sell by date. It doesn't say "woah . . . you are way too needy!" Love is unconditional. Love means we are worthy, and valuable, all of the time. Not in spite of our difficulties, but because of them. The unconditional love from a healthy parent, or long-term partner can be the most wonderful and beautiful thing. But . . . it is the unconditional love that we offer ourselves that will be the most important relationship decision we ever make. We need to love ourselves hard. To not see ourselves as too much, too needy, or a burden. How we treat ourselves gives other people a blueprint for how to treat us. Let's make sure it's a bloody good one.

Reframing the Lie

Instead of this:
~~I am a burden.~~

Try this:
I am a person of value no matter what needs I have.
I deserve kindness and consideration in all my relationships.

"You Are Not a Burden"

Written by Rich

A few weeks into mine and Rox's relationship, she texted me.

"Babe, I really need to speak to you."

My brain immediately went to catastrophe mode: *That's it. She's ending it. I knew it was too good to be true . . .*

We arranged a time to meet, and I could tell she was incredibly nervous and scared. Sat in a Basingstoke pub, clutching my chilled Diet Coke glass, I braced for impact.

"I'm so sorry," she began, "but I have kept something so important from you. I need to share this. And I understand if this changes you wanting to be with me . . ."

My heart was pounding now. This was going to be BAD.

"My credit rating is really awful," she told me, her eyes wide, her hands shaking. In her mind, she had just delivered a killer blow that would end our relationship. I sat there silently, extremely relieved that the news she had delivered was a literal non-issue for me . . . a credit rating? I was in finance! That was incredibly easy to sort out. But she continued.

"I don't want to be the reason we can't get a house in future. I don't want to hold you back. I've been terrible with money my whole life, and I'm so ashamed of where I'm at."

Now, this might be radical, but when I was searching dating apps back in the day, my search criteria definitely didn't look like this:

- 30–40 years of age
- Good sense of humour
- *Must have a good credit rating*

But for Rox, her lack of good credit was a stamp of disapproval from life. A reminder of all of her years struggling to pay bills and curb her spending. It was as if Experian (the UK credit scoring company) had valued *her* personally as "very poor," not just her likelihood to pay back a loan. There was a powerlessness about the way she viewed it, like that label was going to be there forever.

"Babe," I told her, "luckily for you, you've fallen for a bank manager. We'll get you registered to vote. Pay off a few bills. Add your name to the utilities, and you'll have it sorted in no time."

I'm happy to report that Rox's credit rating has moved from very poor to excellent in the time we have been together. And we are considering buying our first home together. We have a really open and flexible way of working with money. And we have some (what some people may think are unusual) ways of managing things together. I've never once seen her financial situation as a burden. To me, it was simply a problem that was relatively easy to fix. Not the end of the world.

To Rox, however, a bad credit rating meant she was unlovable. That she was going to ruin our life together. That there was no saving the situation. This pattern of behaviour, where she struggles with something and then believes she has ruined her entire life because of it, is something I have seen a lot. Buried deep in her bones is a belief that there will be a punishment if she makes an ADHD-related mistake.

This sense that she was unwelcome unless she has zero needs extended way beyond her ADHD struggles. It would be an oversimplification to say that Rox only felt like a burden when she lost something, needed a speedy ride to the train station, or forgot an important date. It affected all areas of her life.

Growing up in a dysfunctional household with undiagnosed ADHD, Rox had learned that all problems were hers to fix alone. She just needed to try harder. Focus more. Not be so unreliable. Not quit things. And be more organized. Any difficulties she faced were the result of her bad actions, nothing more. So many ADHDers grow up in similar environments; it's no wonder they believe they are a burden to the people they love, and who love them too.

The thing is, though—and I won't gloss over it—dating someone with ADHD can be challenging at times. You will need to have tough conversations. You will need to compromise. You will need to learn a totally new way of doing things. You will need to learn what your personal triggers are and how to manage them. Without a thorough understanding of these things, we run the risk of relaying the same message to a partner with ADHD that they have heard over and over: that they aren't valuable unless they change.

I'm only human. As someone who loves a room to be tidy, is always on time, and never forgets anything, living with someone who is the total opposite is going to bring about challenges. It's how we deal with these challenges that will ultimately lead to a healthy or unhealthy relationship. Here's an example of how I got it horribly wrong a few weeks ago.

"Babe," I said to Rox, "we're leaving in five minutes."

Rox put down her phone, then sprang out of bed and into action. "No problemo!" she told me as she sped off.

Five minutes later, she was running round the kitchen in a blind panic, searching for her wallet.

"I swear it was here . . . I'm so sorry!"

I could hear the fear in her voice, see the panic in her movements.

"We're going to miss this goddamn train!" I told her, my voice raised, shaking my head in dismay at her. The minute the words left my body, I knew I could have chosen a different reaction. But I was tired, I'd given her fair warning, and I was worried about being late. Like I said, I'm only human.

"I'll leave it. I don't need it." Rox's tears bubbled to the surface and her face turned bright red. I knew she was struggling. Trying to shut down the massive emotional reaction she was having. But I couldn't comfort her in this moment. I was facing my own pretty strong emotional reaction to being late. We got into the car in silence.

A few deep breaths later, I was ready to have another go.

"Are you okay, bubby?" I asked her, and put my hand on her leg.

'No . . . I'm really struggling. I feel so panicked and lost and stupid. I'm so sorry I couldn't find my wallet again." Her tears were flowing freely now. "And now I'm going to ruin my eye-liner!"

"I'm so sorry I spoke to you that way, babe. That wasn't okay. I promise I'll help you find your wallet when we're back. We've got my card. We'll be okay."

There was a look of instant relief on her face. Just knowing that she hadn't ruined the day. That our plans could go ahead despite a slightly flustered departure. And of course, because of my acknowledgement of the way I had spoken to her.

Nobody is going to get it right all the time. Not me. Not Rox. Not you. Not your parents. Not your partner. Not your kids. Accepting that an ADHD partner is going to piss you off sometimes is actually extremely healthy. There is nothing wrong with getting frustrated. It's how we deal with the frustration.

What isn't okay is to lash out at your ADHDer, and blame them for the anger or frustration that has been evoked in you. And in the moments we do lash out, because we are all human, it's important to say sorry. And really mean it. To hold their hand, look them in the eye, and say, "I let frustration get the best of me. Sorry. You don't deserve to be spoken to like that."

ADHD humans have complex and different needs. Every day may present a different struggle. And every day, we have an opportunity either to let them know they are unwelcome and annoying, or safe and loved. All we can do is try and choose the second option every day.

How to Help an ADHDer
Who Believes They're a Burden

Your ADHDer will likely believe that their needs are too much. That they do not deserve the support that they get. And that asking you for that support is selfish. They have often gone years fighting through life on their own, attempting to fix themselves, failing over and over again, and taken on that shame as a personal failing.

Showing up next to them, to help them and to love them through all of their struggles, is one of the most healing things we can do. It will begin to reverse the narrative that they are unwanted in their natural form, without masking. It takes love and patience to build an environment where your ADHDer can ask for help without feeling immense guilt or shame. But the end results are so worth it. Every human being struggles—with fear, anxiety, pain from childhood, work worries, etc. Both humans in any given relationship deserve love, understanding, support and encouragement.

Here are a few steps you can take:

1. **DON'T IGNORE THE ISSUE**: Pretending like everything they do is totally fine and has no effect on you isn't showing up honestly in the relationship. It's important to share how certain behaviours affect you. Not to blame or shame, but to express your position and take ownership of your own part of an emotional reaction. There are struggles related to having ADHD that a partner will experience. We don't need to sugar-coat it. But we need to let them know their struggles are welcome, and that you are open to working on them all together, ensuring everyone's voice is heard.

2. **USE CO-REGULATION**: Your ADHDer may mask their struggles. We want to provide an environment safe enough for them to allow their true self into the equation. This is particularly important in moments of panic, isolation or meltdown. One of the most helpful things is genuinely asking if they are okay, with no stress or malice behind the question. And offering a hug. A hug is an amazing co-regulation tool. It can help a distressed person's body to calm down from the extreme emotions they may be having. This also shows them we are not afraid of their emotions. If a hug is too intense, just letting them know you are there, and that you love them, is another option.

3. **LEARN SELF-REGULATION**: You will have your own reactions to your partner. You will be angry, frustrated and unloving at times. It's so important to vocalise these feelings. Both people's needs matter equally, no matter the relationship. The trick is to learn to communicate your own feelings, not how the ADHDer has "made you" feel. Using "I" statements can be really helpful here. For example, compare "You made a mess in the bedroom! I'm so angry!" with "I'm feeling a bit frustrated about the mess. Can we chat about how to sort it out?" It's an invitation to solve the problem together rather than just an opportunity to shame them.

4. **USE PATIENCE**: After a lifetime of feeling broken, of feeling like they are the problem, like they deserve their struggles, true warmth and love are going to feel very different. And it will take time for them to accept it. We're in this for the long game. The more we show up in loving and supportive ways, the more they will unmask, trust us with their inner vulnerabilities and struggles, and the more happiness, joy and intimacy you will create in your home.

Reframing the Lie

When they say this:

~~I am a burden.~~

Try telling them this:
You are loved deeply, even when you are struggling.
You are not alone in your struggles.

ADHD Lie #9: I Am a Failure

Written by Rox

My mum died when I had just turned 22, after a three-year battle with cancer. After her death I moved back home to try to recover. After a few weeks in a blur of sleep, grief and shock, I accidentally overheard one of my father's phone calls.

He was explaining how I was at home and so coming here was inconvenient.

The words cut me deeply. It was my dad's love I had always craved so much. He had been my hero growing up. Yet . . . I also felt that I had been an inconvenience to him for many years. My instinct was to get out. To run away.

So, I begged and borrowed my way into a spare room with a friend in London and applied for a job working in the city. I'd dropped out of my accountancy course a few months before—thank God—trust me, nobody wants me doing their taxes.

I knew I wouldn't be able to get another graduate job, having quit the last one after three months, so I applied to be an assistant in an investment bank. The money was good enough to pay the rent on my spare room, and it was relatively easy to get compared to the six-month process I'd gone through to get the elusive "graduate job" I had just left.

Work began at 6 a.m. I literally have no idea how I made that work for as long as I did. I was grieving. Suicidal. And yet somehow more able to stick to a routine than I am now. It was the epitome of masking: covering up my ADHD symptoms, my grief and my loneliness.

It was during my first year there that I wrote a song called "LATE" on my guitar. (My mum's full name was Linda Angela Theresa Emery, so it was named after her. The irony of my first song being about time-keeping though is not lost on me!) It was the only way I was able to get the pain out. I didn't have the option of a supportive family, or even the knowledge of how to use my words to express what was happening inside. Music became the only place where I could express the depths of what I was feeling.

"Jesus, Rox. That is really good. You need to get to an open mic night."

I turned to see my gorgeous, well-spoken, business-minded flatmate Sarah standing in the doorway listening.

"Oh, no. I couldn't do that . . ."

"Rox, it's a must. I'm not taking no for an answer."

Something about her confidence felt like it was easier to agree than to say no. The following Wednesday, I was setting up at the local pub, The Phoenix, to play the three songs I had written. I downed a few pints of cider to take the edge off, and I got up to play. My flatmates and work colleagues had come to cheer me on, and I saw them all looking on proudly.

Sitting hunched over, I stared down at my guitar. I didn't speak to the little crowd of nine. My hands and my voice were shaky despite the booze. Yet . . . it lit something inside me. Something just felt right about singing songs I had written.

Over the next few weeks, I signed up to play a few more open mics. And the craziest thing happened. I was approached by a music manager. This led to a meeting with an investor. And a few months later, I had a record deal.

Those years were a whirlwind:

> Releasing my first single.
> Getting onto the iTunes chart.
> Recording my first album.
> Selling out my first show.
> Touring the UK as a support act for *X Factor* winners.
> Selling out another show.

I was on a path to success, carried by what felt like an invisible energy. Doors just seemed to open. Things just seemed to work out.

And then . . . weeks before the release of my debut album, the record label I was signed to went bust. Everything fell apart overnight.

I tried my best to keep things going with no label, spending money that I had been left by my mum. I burned through thousands and thousands of dollars. But nothing worked. Without the support of a label, I had no clue what I was doing. Throwing money at things, attempting to be the organizational heart of my business. I was drowning. I was still really young at this point, only in my mid-twenties, and still in desperate grief over my mum. And watching this project crumble in front of me broke something inside of me. Music had become my reason to stay alive. To get up and sing songs about losing my mum was the only way to feel okay. To feel close to her. And to feel like my life had some sort of purpose. Losing that was losing a part of myself.

There was nowhere to turn, and nothing to do. I had failed spectacularly . . . or so I thought.

That's it. I am quitting music. I will never ever do this again.

I made a pact with myself. Music was over. I had learned my lesson. I would never let myself be hurt by a dream ever again. I would never *allow* myself to dream again.

What followed was my descent into drugs, alcohol and sex addiction. And that lasted a decade. That story is perhaps best told in another book. But let me try my best to sum it up . . .

Secretly self-harming.
Being blackout drunk most nights.
Addicted to cocaine.
Partying a lot.
Cheating on partners.
Running up debts.
Living in squalor.
Moving from place to place.

In 2018, after a three-night bender in Ibiza, I made the decision to walk into a recovery meeting.

Without alcohol or sex to keep me distracted, the feelings I had been running from my whole life began to bubble to the surface. Okay, more like *erupted* to the surface. I had a mental breakdown in early 2020. I was suffering paranoid delusions, a deep sense that people hated me, were out to get me, and that I wasn't safe. I was hypervigilant, noticing every small detail. A little bit of Doctor Google-ing had me convinced I had borderline personality disorder, or BPD. I found a therapist online and booked an appointment on my credit card.

"I've researched my symptoms and I think I have BPD," I told her. "I would like to know what to do about it. I don't want to dig into family stuff . . . I've made peace with the past. But I need this paranoia and rage to stop."

We began the deep inner work. We used my current triggers to paint a picture of what might be going on. We explored patterns of behaviour, deeply held beliefs. We uncovered patterns of trauma and abuse that dated back to childhood. Some days, I left feeling all I'd done was chat shit for an hour. Some days I left feeling like I'd uncovered something huge. Some days I left swearing to never go back because my therapist had touched on something so painful. But I kept going.

One of the strangest, yet most helpful things I began to practise was a breathing exercise. She explained the science to me:

"Your body is very often in fight-or-flight mode. It doesn't know how to be calm. We can use the breathing exercise to train the body to feel normal in a calm state."

It was the first part of my trauma recovery journey. And something that really did change how I felt in my body. I didn't know your hands weren't meant to shake all the time. I didn't know you didn't need to feel ready to fight or run away at all times.

For anyone interested in trying this exercise, we have included it in our body-doubling app, dubbii. You can download it for free and access the breathing exercise as many times as you like. This is, of course, not a replacement for psychotherapy, but that option is not open to everyone. And of everything I learned and tried, that simple exercise had the biggest impact on my body.

Something began to shift in me. It was not just that I felt more peaceful in body. I was more ready to find a healthy relationship. More present with my emotions. I began to dream again, something I had sworn I would never do.

Once more, I had the desire to try and make it as an artist. To sing my songs again. I began to wonder what would happen if I gave it one more try. Sober. In therapy. Building on the experience of all of the "failures" of my past?

I never felt ready. I never felt good enough. And I still felt incredibly ashamed of my age. Starting an artistic career at 35 is pretty much unheard of in the music industry. Yet . . . I had just enough hope, just enough wonder, just enough desire to try again. (And, so my editor insists, heaps of talent, too!)

I carried my shame, my imposter syndrome, and my belief that it was too late on my back, and I began walking to wherever I needed to be. Into the studio to record a song. Into a meeting to see if someone might want to release it. Into TikTok to test out my writing. I won't lie to you—it was incredibly hard. I was swimming against the current of what I believed to be true. I didn't feel ready. Or worthy. And I was deeply embarrassed that my friends and family would roll their eyes at seeing me "giving music another go."

But I did it anyway.

At the time of writing this, at the grand young age of 39 (109 in music years!), I have just sold out my second tour. I'm playing festivals this year. And I'm working on my debut album, which will likely come out when I am 40. There is no way I could have planned for this. I never expected it. I am constantly gobsmacked that things are working out in a way I truly thought would never be available to me. I hope just as many gifts are awaiting you, too.

To have ADHD means to have a highly active thinking brain. When that brain is starved of its ability to hope for a better future, to dream of a better life, we become stifled. Depressed. Hopeless.

I wonder how many of you reading this have an idea you have always wanted to work on, a creative passion you have given up on, or a vision for your future that feels out of reach. I wonder what it would be like to completely switch your narrative. To no longer believe that it's too late for you.

Years and years of trying to fix ourselves means we are walking around feeling undeserving and incapable. And that is why ADHD acceptance and support are the core foundation to a happy and fulfilling life.

It's time to radically accept what we are not, and to make space to radically accept what we are! My ADHD still rages its way through my life. Sometimes:

I forget to post songs.
I think people hate my work.
I lose things on public transport.
I change my mind often.
I am perfectionistic.

But it doesn't matter. It doesn't stop me. The limitations are there, I am aware of them, and it's okay. I do not need to do everything. I do not need to be struggle free. I simply need to show up and do the best I can to move towards my goal on any given day.

Whatever it is in the back of your mind, begging you to take a chance, I hope that you listen to that voice. I hope you can believe that you may in fact be totally and utterly wrong in your assessment of yourself as a failure. I hope you realise that your low self-esteem is a direct result of living a life with an unsupported medical condition, and that in a different environment, you can flourish in ways you can barely imagine!

To the writers, painters, craft makers, problem solvers, business starters, teachers, and untold other wonderful beings waiting to emerge, may you walk head-first in the direction of your dreams.

Unlearning the "I Am a Failure" Lie

Pretending to fit into a neurotypical world when you have ADHD is a full-time job. It's no wonder so many of us gave up on our dreams. We simply didn't have the time, energy or confidence!

Years may have gone by as we desperately try to stay out of debt, stay in relationships, stay in jobs, and keep a tidy house. And then, one day, we wake up to realise our entire life has passed us by. We've acted our way through it. Pretended to be okay. Denied ourselves. Belittled our gifts. Focused on our flaws. We've allowed the world to make us feel like we are undeserving. Well, fuck that. It is never too late to become who you already are.

Here are a few first steps to get you on that path:

1. **CHALLENGE NEGATIVE BELIEFS**: It's time to stop the inner negative narrative of "I'm too old." "It's too late." "I don't deserve it." This change will not happen immediately. But with consistent action in the direction of your dreams, you will chip away at that narrative and begin to understand that those words simply are not true. They were just a reflection of your historical environment, which was often misunderstood and unsupported. Dream up some happier ones: "What if I made it?" "What if I inspire others?" "What if my experience is my biggest gift?"

2. **ACCEPT THAT FAILURE IS NECESSARY**: The only way to win is to lose. Over and over until you learn the lessons. It is said that it takes ten years to become an overnight success. It takes twenty if you have ADHD! Every misstep up until this point is actually part of the path you needed to walk to gather experience, build resilience, and refine your craft. There is no shame in failure. There is only strength.

3. **DON'T LET YOUR PAST DEFINE YOUR FUTURE**: Struggling to keep a tidy house, not lose your keys, text your friends back, and stay in a job that breaks you to your core. You are left feeling different and bad. Understanding that these are symptoms of ADHD that you can't fix no matter how hard you try is going to buy you so much freedom and time. No wonder it didn't work before: you were drowning, and alone. It's changed now. You understand why you may have struggled; you can make adjustments this time around, and you can have a different experience.

4. **REALISE THAT ACTIONS BEAT WORDS**: You are going to doubt yourself. You are going to be scared. You

are going to think you aren't good enough. You are going to want to quit. DO IT ANYWAY. You do not have to love yourself. Just do what you need to do to get started. You will gain confidence with every single step that you take. So, take the first step, with the faith that things will unfold exactly as they are meant to. When you show up for your natural gifts, over and over again, life will change. You see, we cannot change our ADHD. That's there to stay. But we can dramatically and miraculously change our own lives.

Reframing the Lie

Instead of this:
~~I am a failure.~~

Try this:
Failure is a necessary part of success.
It's the perfect time for me to work on my dreams.

"You're Not a Failure"

Written by Rich

Standing at the back of a sold-out show in Glasgow, I'm watching Rox perform on stage. The crowd is screaming back every lyric. The band are fantastic. She's absolutely in her element.

We're in the middle of her first sold-out tour of the UK. I'm there driving the van, a job I take very seriously, and selling the merchandise.

It's been the most incredible time. I've never travelled like this, or "been on the road," as musicians say. But I'm starting to understand why the life of a touring musician is so often romanticised. Travelling around the country, with a tight-knit group of eight of us. Long drives, cheap hotels, sold-out shows. The camaraderie is a phenomenal experience.

Rox, who performs as RØRY, launches into her last song, "Uncomplicated," a pop-punk banger that lifts the roof off. Six hundred emo fans scream the lyrics back at her. This is the song that changed a lot for Rox. It went viral on TikTok in 2021 and has grown and grown since then. Standing there, watching her, I can't help but feel so proud of her. I've been with her throughout her entire artistic journey. Watching her on stage as she lives out a dream she had long ago given up on. It's nothing short of inspiring.

But getting to this point was one hell of a journey. When Rox and I first met, she was actually embarrassed about her music. On one of our first dates, we were hanging out with a couple of friends of hers, and they suggested Rox play me one of her songs.

"God, no. Not that awful rubbish," she joked, but there was something deeply serious in the undertone. I pushed a couple of times to hear the music she was writing, but she wouldn't play it. She was deeply uncomfortable even being asked.

Eventually, after a few months together, she played me a song. She sat with her head hanging low, eyes darting from side to side. She had the demeanour of someone who was delivering some incredibly awful news, not someone just sharing a piece of art. I truly didn't understand.

"Sounds awesome, babe!" I told her. "You should put it out."

"I can't. It's not good enough. And that would be so embarrassing . . . I'm 35 years old!"

What's interesting about Rox is that all of her words would say she didn't want to release music, that she hated it and felt too old. Yet all of her actions said quite the opposite—that she had a story to tell and was drawn to music over and over again as a way of telling it.

"What's the worst that could happen?"

"It flops. Everybody laughs at me. I fail again. And make a total fool of myself."

"And what's the best that could happen?"

"Umm . . ."

Rox spent hours, days, months, obsessing over the fact she was too old to make music. Convinced she wasn't good enough. That she would make a fool of herself. That "people" would laugh at her. Hello RSD! She never spent any time thinking about the opposite. The possibility that things might work out well! Years and years of living with undiagnosed (and, perhaps more importantly, unsupported ADHD) had wrecked her self-esteem.

When she looked in the mirror, she saw someone who was broken.

I wonder how many other people's dreams have been stolen this way? How many ADHDers who had great talents and passions gave up because they believed they didn't deserve it, or weren't good enough, or whatever other lies they'd absorbed over a lifetime of getting things wrong.

"I'll help you," I told her. "We can do it together. You'll be okay."

Those early months after Rox made the decision to release music again were interesting in our house ... Budget photoshoots were taking place one day, mixes were blasted in the car, and Rox was regularly breaking down in tears. The more she started to actually commit, the more the fear became a reality: she was really doing it. She was opening herself up to the possibility of failure and rejection again. The sensitivities of an ADHDer make this a painful experience. I have the true joy of not caring at all what people think of me. It's incredibly freeing! But Rox was operating with a crippling sense of certainty that she would fall flat on her face, and everyone would laugh at her.

But she kept going. She even made the extremely odd decision (or so it seemed to me at the time) to join TikTok. She was so embarrassed by herself that she joined under a joke name @punkrockgirl, with the aim of writing little joke skits about the life of a musician. A perfect way to dip her toe in the water, but under the guise of comedy, so if it failed it wouldn't really hurt. Soon her confidence grew as she moved away from the eyes of friends and family and that imaginary judgmental figure witnessing her every move. Emboldened, she began uploading little clips of her singing. Soon came her first viral video, "Psychological War," a song about the abuse she went through with a family member.

After a time, she changed her account name to @its_r_o_r_y and simply began sharing her songs. One clip at a time. Soon another song, "Uncomplicated," went viral. Doors started to open. And, even with her still-shaky self-belief, Rox walked through them. This led her to her first sold-out gig, then a tour, then the release of two EPs, and at the time of writing, two years since her first single came out, she is heading off on tour again, playing festivals, and working on her debut album.

I've watched her confidence grow and grow, directly in proportion to how much she was able to show up. She has been relentlessly chipping away at the belief she was too old / too cringe / too whatever, and now she's just an artistic person making art. I don't think you can get happier than that.

Undiagnosed ADHD stifled Rox's confidence. It made her feel like a fraud, incapable of achieving anything. After all, if you can't do your laundry, or if you keep losing your keys, how will you *ever* do something of value? All of her struggles had been labelled as failure, but through an ADHD lens, those struggles made sense, and they were easy to accept and support. Diagnosis allows people deep in self-hatred to loosen the grip that shame and self-loathing have on them. To begin to unwind a lifetime of believing they are broken and understand that they are deserving of love and support. In that new environment, the ADHDer can thrive.

So let me bring you back to where I am now. I'm watching her jump up and down on stage, screaming the lyrics to her biggest song. Smiling. Alive. Quite literally living her best life. She's up there because she dared to try again, after never, ever believing she would be here. But it didn't matter: the world rewards those who show up and face their fears. It's that simple.

How to Help an ADHDer Who Believes They're a Failure

It's a bit of an old cliché that ADHD kids are told at school: "You've got potential, but you don't try!" Yet another message these kids get, from the world at large, is that they are personally at fault for their struggles. As ADHDers struggle to live up to this "potential," and to even survive in this world, they lose all faith in themselves. The thing is, though, that potential is still there. That spark that makes them different. It may have been dulled by a world that has made them feel broken, but it will never be fully extinguished.

So many adults are now figuring out that they have ADHD and suddenly realising why life has been so hard. And they're mourning the life they could have had. Grieving the hard years they have had to fight to make it through. It's an important part of the process. And so is dreaming. And hoping—that their talents, interests, creativity and potential can be realised. An ADHDer who is supported and encouraged is capable of creating beautiful worlds for themselves and others.

Here are some ways to help with this process:

1. **QUESTION THE NARRATIVE**: If your ADHDer has a creative endeavour, business idea, or life purpose lying dormant because of negative beliefs, it's important to get to the root cause. Ask them questions about their choices, their lack of belief in themselves, their worries. You can then kindly reflect that perhaps things are not quite as bad as they seem. And that things can actually work out really well for them.

2. **OFFER SUPPORT WHERE YOU CAN**: If you have the time, and are in a position to do so, offer to help them with admin—the little behind-the-scenes details that are essential to getting projects off the ground, but with which your ADHDer probably struggles. This can be life-changing to an ADHDer. Removing the burden of having to work in areas they really struggle with allows them to double-down on where their talents lie. Not only does this build self-esteem very quickly, it will also bring results.

For years ADHDers have been trying and failing to fix themselves. Imagine the relief when they try to do something that they are gifted at and find that, with the foundations taken care of, it's actually possible.

3. **WATCH OUT FOR OVERTHINKING**: Perfectionism can kill a lot of ADHD projects and ideas. Often, people with ADHD feel that if it's not the best, it's the worst. They may have used perfectionism as a way to avoid harsh criticism, which they find intolerable. Having a free space for them to vent their innermost thoughts to you, particularly highly critical or perfectionistic ones, will allow you to reflect back reality to them, that "done is better than perfect." That they can't fail. That all they need to do is take the next step.

4. **STOP COMPARISON IN ITS TRACKS**: ADHDers will often compare themselves with others, in an attempt to justify that something is wrong with them. Or that they are making mistakes. As your ADHDer begins to take strides towards their dreams, they will no doubt begin to compare themselves to others who are on different journeys. Gently but firmly bring them back into their own story, into reality, where their actions can change their outcomes. Comparison is the thief of joy.

Reframing the Lie

When they say this:

~~I am a failure.~~

Try telling them this:
You have a lot you can add to this world.
You don't have to do it alone.

ADHD Lie #10: The World Would Be Better Off Without Me

Written by Rox

Lying in the spare room at my friend's house, I felt a wave of calm wash over me. I made a silent pact with myself. One that would allow me to escape the daily Groundhog Day of constant failures and mounting shame.

The day Dad dies, I'm going too.

It's a small, quiet thought. Which seems so odd, given its gargantuan consequences. There would be no fanfare. No big deal made. No mess made. Just me, leaving quietly, with a bottle of pills.

I had lost my mum to cancer almost fourteen years prior. The experience had torn the heart right out of me, and it had never quite grown back, like a bullet hole in my chest. Grief is a brutal, complicated experience. It's known that grief can amplify ADHD symptoms,[12] and so in the years after my mother's death, with no support for either that or my ADHD, every aspect of my life had utterly fallen apart. I had stacked shame upon shame until I couldn't carry the weight anymore.

But lying there that night, I could finally breathe. I knew that I wouldn't be able to cope with the death of my dad. I wasn't strong enough to go through it again. But I also wouldn't put him through losing me. So, I would go on as long as I could, rally against the darkness for a few more years, and then I would leave this place knowing I'd put in a good effort after all.

Sure, the odd friend would miss me for a while. But they would be okay within a few weeks. There was nobody left who would be utterly heartbroken by my departure. I had no real family of my own; I was always appearing as a bit part in someone else's story. Always the extra seat at someone else's Christmas dinner. The guest in the spare room of someone else's family home. I didn't add anything to this world. In fact, I had taken rather a lot away from it.

Every lie I had ever told, every person I'd hurt or let down, every bill that went unpaid, every dream that went unrealised was just more evidence of the fact that I didn't really belong here. That the world would be better off without me.

A recent study by Henry Shelford states that adults with ADHD are five times more likely to have attempted suicide than those without it.[13] That's a *500 percent* greater chance of taking our own lives. I want you to think about that for a moment. How is it that this condition, one that most see primarily as an issue of "paying attention," could be linked to people not wanting to be here anymore? Surely not being able to stay on task is by no means grounds for someone believing that the world would be better off without them in it.

When I look back on myself in 2019, it breaks my heart that I could so calmly and quietly make such a devastating decision without so much as a flinch. That it felt like such a welcome resolve to a life of constant failure. Taken alone, the symptoms of ADHD really don't sound that serious, not in the grand scheme of things. But it isn't the symptoms that lead to suicidal thoughts. It's their consequences and the beliefs that we form about ourselves as a result.

For example, impulsiveness. Taken on its own, it doesn't sound like a symptom that will play out to lead somebody to the darkest corners of this world. But let's look a little deeper.

Say somebody with undiagnosed ADHD struggles with impulsive spending. They rack up credit card debts that they find difficult to pay. They struggle to stay on top of the bills and end up falling into arrears. Bailiffs show up at their door. There is now a legal case against them and they must show up in court. And that's how something as seemingly small as impulsiveness can end up shattering a life.

Now let us consider somebody who often loses and misplaces things. Again—surely everybody does this? Not that big a deal, right? But let's look at someone with undiagnosed ADHD who has a habit of losing things. Say they are due to fly out to America for a once-in-a-lifetime work opportunity—only the night before, they lose their passport. They end up missing their flight, letting down everybody they were due to meet and work with, and ultimately losing their job. In this way, "losing things" can become dark very quickly for someone with ADHD.

Let's take somebody who has difficulty with admin and with organizing tasks. Again, no big deal. They may have a pile of unopened letters, but how bad can that really be? Now, let's look at someone who has been unable to attend a routine smear test for ten years because they have not been able to organize the doctor's appointment. Let's imagine that they have a family history of cervical cancer. Again, suddenly we can see how everything escalates fast.

All these examples are me, by the way.

ADHD is so often seen by others as a condition that isn't really that serious. And this in turn leads to the incorrect conclusion that those suffering with it aren't really suffering at all. They are simply refusing to get better, to do basic tasks, and bringing all of their struggles on themselves because they simply won't live a normal, respectable life. And herein lies the absolute biggest problem: when somebody with ADHD feels judged for being inferior and feels that they themselves are at fault for their symptoms, they will have no one to turn to when things get dark. They will feel like they do not deserve help, because they've brought this on themselves.

And this is why we need to talk about where ADHD can lead, at its worst. We need more research on *why* we are more likely to commit suicide, and more early interventions to stop kids growing up in the grip of the horrendous internal beliefs that we have discussed in this book.

If you are reading this book and feel you are currently in the darkest of places, I encourage you with everything I have to seek help. I can promise there are people out there who care so deeply about you. Perhaps an old friend, family member, or somebody you haven't even met yet. In the middle of darkness, it becomes impossible to see the light, but I promise you it is still there. Although this world can be full of sadness and pain, it is equally full of beauty and love. If you are reading this book, and you have made it through your darkest times, survived an attempt, or built a life you love from a place of hopelessness, please share your story. Shout it from the rooftops, in any way you can. One of the most humbling things about surviving is that you now have a roadmap to show others how to do it too.

Reflecting on the chapters in this book, and the deep places that they have taken me as I've looked back on my own life during the writing, I can better understand why there is such a great risk to life for those with ADHD. Let's think for a second about the core beliefs covered in this book, beliefs that were highlighted by our community. Imagine what it is like to live with a constant narrative playing in your head, like a broken record playing over and over, repeating:

- **I am lazy.**
- **I'm not trying hard enough.**
- **I quit everything I start.**
- **I am stupid.**
- **I am a bad person.**
- **Everybody secretly hates me.**
- **I am useless.**
- **I am a burden.**
- **I am a failure.**
- **The world would be better off without me.**

What do we expect is going to happen? Do we think we can believe these things about ourselves and somehow still live happily? That this kind of relentless shame and bullying will somehow uncover our best selves? Suicidal ideation and suicide attempts are the expression of a deep hopelessness. The fruit of a poisoned tree. That tree is first poisoned by the outside world, and as we grow up, we start to do the poisoning ourselves. We have absorbed the negative messages around us, and taken up the torch to continue to rebroadcast them internally. In order to heal and move forward, we *must* weed out the toxic core beliefs that have poisoned our lives for so long. We need to dig them up, understand them, and then burn them. And then we must replace them instead with the truth.

The truth looks something like this:

- **I don't need to "fix" myself.**
- **I am multi-passionate.**
- **I deserve to work at a job I enjoy.**

- **It's okay to change direction.**
- **I struggle with certain things due to my condition.**
- **I also have lots of skills that others don't have.**
- **I sometimes need extra reassurance, and that is okay.**
- **I am a person of value no matter what needs I have.**
- **It isn't too late for me to follow my dreams.**
- **I deserve to be here.**

The fruit of this tree is very different. It is not poisoned or rotting. Quite the opposite, in fact: it is covered in beautiful, vibrant blossoms. When we change our core beliefs, we change the roots of that tree that we build our very lives on. Change the roots, change the tree.

For so long, I was trapped in trying to change the "blossoms" of my life. The problems I could see. My lack of discipline. My terrible finances. My relationship struggles. I was fumbling around trying to fix what was visible, while the true cause of my suffering remained buried under the surface. It wasn't until the toxic core beliefs were weeded out and changed that my efforts to become someone I was proud of were able to come to fruition.

I think back to the hopeless 2019 me, quietly resigned to leaving this planet early, and I want to say the following to her:

Kid, you stuck around. You walked shakily through your worst days with nobody beside you. Although you believed you were broken beyond repair, you held onto the tiniest spark of hope that not even the cruellest of critics could extinguish. The hope that perhaps, somehow, underneath it all, you did have something to offer this world . . . You walked yourself into therapy and began the years and years of work to unpack all of the difficulties that had plagued your life and relationships. You took accountability for some of the behaviours that had hurt other people, and yourself. And you finally began to see yourself as someone of value for the first time.

This book would not exist without your bravery. Without your decision to stay with us. You had no idea where we were going to end up . . . I wish I could tell you about Rich and Lillie and Seer. About our house, and about our lives together, which are so full of happiness! But you will find out for yourself in a matter of months. Life-changing love is just on the horizon, waiting for you right in the moment you thought it wouldn't ever happen.

Keep going.

Unlearning the "World Would Be Better Off Without Me" Lie

We live in a world where mental health advice so often starts, and stops, with "It's okay to not be okay" and "It's good to talk." Although these statements are often made with the best of intention, they are nowhere near enough. Who exactly am I supposed to talk to, when everyone around me thinks I am the cause of my own struggles? How am I supposed to be "okay" with not wanting to be here anymore?

If you have thought about leaving, about taking your own life, I want you to know you are not alone. There is no thought that you have had that hasn't been had by a great many of us. There is nothing you have done that could ever warrant the punishment of not being here. No matter how far gone you think you are, how irredeemable, there is *always* hope. There is always a chance to utterly turn things around. This does not happen by trying harder. By pretending to be okay. Or by masking the pain. It starts by walking head first into who we truly are. Allowing our struggles and pain to be felt.

We must become our own champion. We must weed out the core beliefs that have grown inside us, and replace them with alternatives that offer truth, acceptance and love. It is not an easy task. It is perhaps the work of a lifetime. But each step you take back towards your true self is a remarkable feat. An act of ADHD advocacy. May you find your voice, your value and your strength in this world, so that you may offer others who are still trapped the road map back home.

Here are some things you will need to help you on that journey:

1. **BRAVERY**: Seek out and find the support that you need. Perhaps this is professional help, talk therapy, group meetings. Perhaps it is as simple as sharing, over a coffee with a trusted friend or colleague, how lost and lonely you are feeling inside. When words are spoken out loud, and truly listened to, they begin to lose their power over us. We can see them for what they are—lies—and begin to change the narrative. You deserve support with your struggles.

2. **HOPE**: No matter how bad things are, no matter how strong your belief that things will not get better, you must reach out for hope. Allow yourself to believe that things can change. Put your incredible imagination to use, not by imagining the worst, but the best possible outcomes for your life. When you get the support and understanding you have been denied for so long and begin to look at life, and yourself, through a different lens, everything will change. There is nothing in your life that cannot be forgiven, restored and accomplished.

3. **COMMUNITY**: Isolation is a particular kind of torture. To see others succeeding where we fail, over years, can lead to a sense of other-ness, a sense that we are outsiders, trapped in a prison without community spirit, shared values, or mutual understanding. Building community for yourself

that includes other neurodivergent people will bring a sense of true understanding into your life. Consider joining some online communities, or perhaps arranging your own group meetings. Do whatever you need to do to feel more normal and less alone in this world.

4. **LOVE**: Love is perhaps the most potent medication for a host of difficulties. It can, of course, come in many forms, but it will always look something like this: an unrelenting reflection of your deep value, worth and purpose in this world. That is what it feels like to be loved. It is what we look for in our deepest friendships and our most profound relationships. It is also how we must begin to view and treat ourselves. The words and stories we repeat in our own minds can either remind us of our flaws, or of our value. We must start speaking to ourselves as if we care. We must learn to big ourselves up.

No more small talk.

Reframing the Lie

Instead of this:
~~The world would be better off without me.~~

Try this:
I deserve to be here.
I am valuable and loved, and I have much to contribute to the world.

"The World Needs You. You Deserve to Be Here"

Written by Rich

"I was going to kill myself tonight anyway."

My 16-year-old raised their head from the toilet bowl where they were repeatedly vomiting. I didn't have time to process the words. I was more focused on keeping them upright so they didn't smash their head on the bathroom floor.

They had arrived at my flat a couple of hours earlier. They spent weekends with me, and Monday to Friday with their mum. We had a good routine going on, and Friday nights were always our nights for a few beers and video games. Seer and I were really close; it was perhaps more of a friendship than a traditional parent / child relationship.

But what I didn't know was that this particular Friday, they had downed half a bottle of their stepdad's whisky before coming to my place. It wasn't until we were cracking open our second beer that I realised something was wrong. Seer stood up to walk to the bathroom and seemed to no longer have control of their legs. They stumbled down the hallway, ricocheting off the walls, and crashed into the bathroom.

I raced in after them and cleared the bathroom of any sharp or glass objects as I realised they weren't able to control themselves at all. They were like a bull in a china shop. The bull was also vomiting down themselves. I held their head up and rubbed their back as they began to puke up about 50 quids' worth of Scotland's finest, and as I knelt there, I thought, "They said they were going to kill themselves." The words hadn't registered at first. It was such a strange thing to say, and it's not something you would ever imagine hearing from your child.

Yet it was the only thing they *could* say, other than the intermittent groans in between bouts of vomiting.

After about an hour, Seer was feeling a bit better, although still completely out of it. I took them to bed and set the obligatory pint of water and sick bowl next to them. I went back to the living room to finish my own beer and think over what had just happened. Their words were spinning in my head. *How the hell am I supposed to react to that?*

The following morning, after a Lucozade and two acetaminophen, Seer was returning to vague human form.

"Last night you said something quite concerning," I began. "You said you wanted to kill yourself. Is that how you feel?"

"No!" They laughed, shaking their head. "No way, man. I was just wasted. I don't feel like that at all."

And that's where we left it. I believed what they were telling me, and part of me was probably very relieved there wasn't any other action I needed to take. Quite frankly, I felt utterly unprepared to have conversations about suicide. There is no parenting advice for what to do with a vomiting and suicidal teen. I was glad we were through it, and I hoped we would never have to speak about it again.

Looking back on that morning now, with everything I have learned through therapy, and with everything I now know, through Rox, about the deep pain neurodivergence can bring, I realise there was so much more going on. And that I could have done so much better. Parenting is a hard gig. I carry a lot of regrets about the way things were. Even when I was drinking, and not as emotionally available as I am now, I can confidently say I did my best, but these days my best is better.

I can see that there was an element of truth in what Seer was saying. That in their totally wasted state they were sharing something with me and letting me see quite how much they were full of self-loathing. Seer had been diagnosed with Asperger's in 2010, now falling under the diagnosis ASD, Autism Spectrum Disorder. Seer struggled a lot with school, and ended up missing a lot of secondary education. Even by this age though, Seer had developed a mask. Like they were pretending to be so much more okay than they truly were. If you asked them if they were okay, they would always say yes, and I would take that at face value. Taking somebody's mask at face value can of course be very dangerous . . .

It truly wasn't until I met Rox a few months later that I would begin to understand Seer's struggle. As I heard Rox describe a suicide attempt she had survived at 22, and the pact she had made with herself at 34, I began to connect the dots. I'm sure none of Rox's friends knew how she was feeling. Most of them thought of her as a very positive and upbeat person. Yet here she was explaining to me she had fully accepted that she was going to end things after her dad passed away.

I realised that there was this river of hopelessness that both Rox and Seer swam in. Both were carrying this heavy weight of never fitting in, and never really being wanted. It's alarming how damaging that can be on a core level. It's why talking about the core beliefs that can develop for neurodivergents is a matter of urgency, and why we, as parents, must learn the skills to talk deeply with our kids and let them know they are valuable.

Looking back on Seer's life, I can see how many times I'd got it wrong, without meaning to. How many times I had reinforced the idea that they were lazy, or just needed to try harder. That's because I didn't know better. I could only see through my own lens, and I had no way to understand the autistic experience. In more recent times, Seer has been able to be a lot more open about their mental health, and about the negative core beliefs that they hold.

Over dinner a few months ago, we ran them through the chapter titles and topics we were planning to write about in this book.

"Tick. Tick. Tick. That's the first test I've got one hundred per cent on," Seer joked in their usual brand of monotone comedy.

I have no doubt they will label this book extremely cringe, and won't be reading it, but who knows? Perhaps they will pick it up one day. And if they do, I want them to know how deeply loved they are by me. How amazing I think they are. And how sorry I am for not seeing how much anguish they were in earlier.

Going on the journey of this book has shocked the hell out of me. I was, and am, astounded by how much more work there is to do for this community. How so many of the solutions offered don't come anywhere near touching the most damaging parts of their experience. It still feels like society's primary goal is to stuff neurodivergent people into a neurotypical mould. The focus always seems to be on how to make them more productive. But what is more important: that someone learns how to clean their room every day, or that someone learns to accept themselves and ask for help where they need it?

Seer and Rox have a lot of similarities. One of them is the utterly feral way they both stack a dishwasher, but they are both also nearly identical in their automatic belief that something is wrong with them.

For me, living in a house with two neurodivergents is an interesting experience. It's messy, it's emotional, it's hilarious, and it's wonderful.

As I reflect on this book, I want to thank you so much for being here with us. For letting us talk to you about our lives, and the ways that we make it work. I want to talk specifically to the partners and parents of neurodivergent people. To say how amazing it is that you are reading this book. Even that is such a powerful act of love for the person in your life. I imagine if more people were, like you, truly interested in learning how to support neurodivergent people from childhood, we wouldn't be dealing with so much cripplingly low self-esteem and the core beliefs Rox and I have spoken about in this book.

I know it can sometimes be hard to know what to do, or how to help. And it can be difficult to make sure that your own needs are looked after at the same time, to ensure that your stories and goals and emotions are just as much part of the equation as theirs. I want you to know it's okay to get annoyed. To want things to be different. We are human beings. We are programmed with our own expectations and desires, and we all have our own experiences, struggles and anxieties. The most powerful work I have done to be a better partner and dad is actually not learning about Rox and my kids, but rather facing my own challenges, which were getting in the way of real emotional connection. My decision to get sober in 2020, and to pursue therapy to help me process being sexually abused as a child, helped me to be able to feel things a lot more deeply, and to connect with my kids and partner on a more profound level.

Sometimes it is only by going to the depths of our own pain that we are able to be there for somebody else's.

How to Help an ADHDer Who Believes the World Would Be Better Off Without Them

The world constantly reminds neurodivergent people of everything they are doing wrong. We must be the person reminding them of what they are doing *right*, and what they are capable of. Our job is to love the person who is in front of us, and not a version of them that we wish they were because it might make things easier for us.

Here's how:

1. **MODEL VULNERABILITY**: Your neurodivergent likely has a very strong mask, one that they have developed over years of pretending to be okay so as not to be a burden. You will need to look beyond their words to really know if they are okay. The best way to do this is to model your own vulnerability. This will help create a safe place where you can both open up, ask for help, and be there for each other.

2. **ENCOURAGE HONESTY**: I truly believe that honesty will change the foundations of your relationship with your neurodivergent. I don't mean being honest about the practical stuff like when they have booked in a music video; I mean the honesty to open up about your own internal world so that they can be honest about their own. You will need to notice when something is not right with them and become the safest space in the world for them to share with you what's really going on.

3. **LOVE**: This is the most underrated and most potent of forces. Cuddles. Joy in each other's company. Unconditional

support. These are the things that provide a foundation for your neurodivergent to start opening up about some of their more difficult thoughts and feelings. When these thoughts are expressed, they can be dealt with together, as a team, so they don't have to go on alone anymore believing something is wrong with them.

4. **BIG TALK**: Talk them up. Tell them you love them. Tell them you are proud of them. Call it out if they speak down to themselves or say something mean about themselves. We have learned in this book the 10 beliefs that are holding them back. The small talk that has been playing in their heads for a lifetime. It's time for BIG TALK. For them to feel valued and understood.

Reframing the Lie

When they say this:

~~The world would be better off without me.~~

Try telling them this:

You are so loved, needed and valuable.
You do not have to do this alone.

One Last Thing:
The Truth About ADHD

Written by Rox & Rich

Phew . . . you just made it through a LOT of "small talk." We hope it wasn't as painful as a well-meaning neurotypical staring into your eyes on Monday morning and asking about your weekend.

Whether one chapter, or all ten, resonated with you, we truly hope this book has made you reflect. That perhaps the worst symptom of ADHD isn't the constant losing things, struggles with time, or over-whelm with work. But it is, in fact, the crippling sense of self-hatred we have developed because of how the outside world has treated these symptoms. For so many of us our goal in life has been to wipe out our ADHD symptoms. To beat them into submission. To find a new hack, or a tool, in order to finally rid ourselves of these parts. Parts we deem unacceptable.

The truth? ADHD is part of who we are. The fabric of our being. Despising it so deeply means we are despising ourselves. I despised myself for decades. I can promise you it is a sure-fire way not to change a thing, but to stay stuck. Bullying is never the way to make meaningful change. How can we find peace when we are constantly at war with ourselves?

So it is finally time to accept exactly who we are.

THE FUNDAMENTAL ADHD TRUTH IS . . .

We're a bit fucking chaotic. And a hell of a lot of lovable.

We hope this book can be the start of your journey to loving yourself. Love doesn't need to be denied until you are finally on top of the washing, haven't lost your headphones in a while, or have no texts to get back to. Self-love can start right now, with the simple decision to never ever again talk down to yourself. To leave the "small talk" behind, and opt to **big yourself up instead**. We leave you with the "big talk manifesto"—a pact that we hope you can make with yourself, and come back to whenever you need it.

Big Talk Manifesto

- I will never call myself horrible names, out loud, or in my own head. If I ever do because I am frustrated or angry, I will apologise to myself.
- I will never let anybody else call me horrible names. I will limit contact with people who make me feel less than.
- I will be vulnerable and tell loved ones what is really going on for me.
- I will think deeply before saying "yes." Making sure I am not people-pleasing or over-extending, but truly because it is something I want to do.
- I will allow my emotions the space they need. The tears and the pain are welcome here.
- I will not make promises to people to "try harder." I will instead explain that some things are harder for me and negotiate a relationship or system that works.
- I will never shame myself for being multi-passionate! I will allow myself to have fun with different hobbies and interests.
- I will walk bravely in the direction of my dreams knowing that with great bravery comes great success!
- I will stop trying to follow the neurotypical path to success, and instead I will follow my heart and my intuition knowing that there is always something valuable to learn.
- I will ask for reassurance from safe people if I am feeling anxious about our relationship.
- I will be patient with myself and allow myself time to learn and grow.

- I will have faith in my future. Knowing that with the right support I have incredible gifts to offer this world.
- I will take the washing out of the dryer. (Sorry . . . couldn't resist.)

Thank you so much for spending this time with us. We have laughed and cried (okay . . . it's mainly Rox that did the crying!). We hope that this was a cup of tea, a warm hug. And possibly . . . the kick in the ass you needed.

So much love,
Rich & Rox

Thank You

First up, to . . . my wonderful ADHD! There's no way I could have written this book without you. From the initial idea, to the many late night hyperfocus sessions to get this done. Thanks for being there guiding this process every step of the way.

To our incredible "ADHD Love" community. Thank you for being on this journey with us. It is your comments and messages that keep us going, and keep us creating. We absolutely love hearing about how our stories have impacted you and your loved ones.

To Marianne and Jen, the editors who have worked with us on this book. Thank you for your patience and diligence, in the face of many late deadlines and changing ideas, you found a way to make sense of the madness. This book would not exist without your careful and considered creativity. Thank you for carrying it with us.

To Oscar and Mark, our agent and manager. For crossing the i's and dotting the t's. (See, that's why we need you!) Thank you for your feedback and guidance every step and mis-step of the way.

Thank you to Dr. Tej, who guided us both through so much over the last few years. So much of what we learned from you fills these pages. In one hour a week you have helped us to transform our lives.

To Seer and Lillie, who no doubt think this book is the most cringe thing ever . . . thank you for bearing with us whilst we filled many a family dinner conversation with "book talk." Thank you for bouncing ideas around with us, and more importantly, showing us that love really is the only thing we need. We love you both so, so very much.

ADHD Dictionary

ADHD TAX: The extra expenses due to memory loss, forgetfulness, or executive dysfunction challenges. Things like buying multiple pairs of headphones, or being unable to return clothes that don't fit.

AuDHD: When somebody is diagnosed with (or highly suspects) they have both autism and ADHD.

BODY-DOUBLING: Where an ADHD person has company during a difficult task, allowing them to get the job done! This may be a friend or family member simply sitting with them, or having somebody on FaceTime!

COMORBIDITY: Illnesses and disorders that often occur alongside ADHD or other mental health disorders.

CPTSD (COMPLEX POST-TRAUMATIC STRESS DISORDER): A condition where you experience symptoms of PTSD such as flashbacks and trauma triggers, as well as difficulty controlling your emotions, and feeling very angry and distrustful towards the world.

DOOM PILES: When you are meant to be tidying up, but you just end up leaving piles all over the house.

DOPAMINING: Mining for dopamine, usually in the form of over-spending on the internet or researching your new favourite hobby.

FEARLEADER: Speaking horribly about yourself, either in your own head, or out loud.

FLOORDROBE: A floor space, usually carpet, that is also used as a wardrobe.

GROY: The equal parts of grief and joy experienced with an ADHD diagnosis.

HIDY UP: When you decide to hide things in bags, or under the bed, instead of actually tidying up.

HYPERFOCUS: The intense focus experienced by those with ADHD where they can concentrate on a particular task for hours on end.

HYPERVIGILANCE: A state often associated with CPTSD, where a person is acutely aware of minute details in their surroundings and feels constantly on edge and unsafe.

MASKING: Pretending to be neurotypical. This can look like covering up ADHD symptoms and acting like everything is okay, which causes a great amount of stress.

NEUROSPICY: A fun term to describe those of us in the neuro-divergent community!

NOTIVATION: The inability to either begin or complete a low dopamine task.

PANIC LEAVING: When stress is high due to lost items and time-management problems, causing an ADHDer to experience high stress when trying to leave the house.

REGULATION CUDDLE: When somebody wraps their arms around you to help you calm down from very intense emotions, particularly in times of high stress.

RSD (REJECTION SENSITIVE DYSPHORIA): The intense, almost physical pain that ADHDers feel when they suffer real or perceived rejection.

SIDE QUEST: When you are meant to be doing something, and go off and start doing something else without telling anybody.

TO GET ADHD'D: When your ADHD wins the battle! Perhaps you lost something important, went to the wrong place, or spent all day in paralysis.

WEAR-AGAIN SHELF: Clothes that an ADHDer does not want to hang up with clean clothes, but that do not yet belong in the dirty washing!

References and Notes

1   Abigail Fagan, "3 Common Negative Core Beliefs of People with ADHD", *Psychology Today*, Nov. 29, 2022, psychologytoday. com/gb/blog/the-reality-gen-z/202211/3-common-negative-core-beliefs-people-adhd

2   Nichole Currie, "What Is Rejection Sensitive Dysphoria, and Why Does It Impact People with ADHD?", WHYY.org, April 27, 2023, whyy.org/segments/what-is-rejection-sensitive-dysphoria-and-why-does-it-impact-people-with-adhd/

3   Larry Silver, MD, "Executive Dysfunction, Explained!", *ADDitude*, Feb. 17, 2022, additudemag.com/executive-function-disorder-adhd-explained/

4   Dr. Oscar D'Agnone, MD, "Recognizing the Strengths of ADHD: Unearthing the Positive Traits", The OAD Clinic, Oct. 4, 2023, theoadclinic.com/post/recognizing-the-strengths-of-adhd-unearthing-the-positive-traits

5   Janice Rodden, "What Is Executive Dysfunction? Signs and Symptoms of EFD", *ADDitude*, Jan. 14, 2021, additudemag. com/what-is-executive-function-disorder/

6   Ellen Littman, Ph.D. with Eve Kessler, Esq., "ADHD: BEHIND THE Behavior", SmartKids, n.d., smartkidswithld.org/getting-help/adhd/adhd-behind-behavior/

7   Rakesh Magon and Ulrich Müller, "ADHD with comorbid substance use disorder: review of treatment", Cambridge University Press Online, Jan. 2, 2018, cambridge.org/core/journals/advances-in-psychiatric-treatment/article/adhd-with-comorbid-

substance-use-disorder-review-of-treatment/C0B6C471528932
F7402424742F0AA463

8   St Pauls Chambers (no author), "What Happens If You Drive
    Without a License", Nov. 28, 2022, stpaulschambers.com/what-
    happens-if-you-drive-without-a-licence/

9   Paul L. Morgan et al., "Racial and Ethnic Disparities in ADHD
    Diagnosis from Kindergarten to Eighth Grade", *Pediatrics*, July
    2013; 132(1): 85–93, ncbi.nlm.nih.gov/pmc/articles/PMC3691530/

10 Devon Frye, "The Children Left Behind", *ADDitude*, Mar. 31,
    2022, additudemag.com/race-and-adhd-how-people-of-color-get-
    left-behind/

11 Megan Anna Neff, "Rejection Sensitive Dysphoria", Neurodiver-
    gent Insights, n.d., neurodivergentinsights.com/blog/rejection-
    sensitive-dysphoria

12 "Handling Grief and Loss when You Have ADHD", Edge
    Foundation, n.d., edgefoundation.org/handling-grief-and-loss-
    when-you-have-adhd/

13 University of Glasgow (no author), "New Study to Understand
    the Relationship Between ADHD and Suicide Risk", Sept. 27,
    2022, gla.ac.uk/news/archiveofnews/2022/september/headline_
    881944_en.html

About the Authors

Roxanne Pink is a platinum-selling songwriter, having written three UK top-ten hits in the last three years. She is also an artist, releasing her own music and touring under the name RØRY. Rox was diagnosed with ADHD in 2021, which has been a life-changing discovery!

Creating content as the neurodiverse half of @ADHD_Love, she is passionate about helping others reach the same acceptance she has found. She is five and a half years sober.

Richard Pink is the neurotypical half of @ADHD_Love, where they have over 200 million global views raising awareness about ADHD. He is the father of two children, Seer and Lillie.

He worked for twenty years as a leader in one of the UK's largest banks, with extensive experience in managing a diverse team and helping colleagues to reach their potential.

Rich and Rox live in Sevenoaks with their family.

Also by
Richard and Roxanne Pink

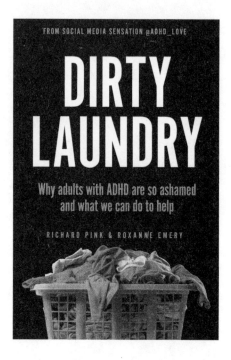

In *Dirty Laundry*, life partners Richard Pink and Roxanne Pink unapologetically guide you through the ups and downs of life with ADHD. Every chapter starts with a common symptom of ADHD, like impulsivity or struggles with finances, and an earnest moment from their own lives to show you how they navigate the symptom together. Rox reminds you to be kind to yourself and love yourself for who you are; Rich offers tips on how he uses compassion and honesty instead of jumping to conclusions. Whether it's helping your ADHDer with friendly time-checks before an appointment or reminding yourself to take breaks during hours spent hyperfocusing on a new project, Rox and Rich give you the tools to destigmatize and normalize life with ADHD.

Available from Ten Speed Press wherever books are sold.
www.tenspeed.com